100

GREAT
LEADING THROUGH
FRUSTRATION
IDEAS

Dr Peter Shaw

Marshall Cavendish
Business

Published by Marshall Cavendish Business
An imprint of Marshall Cavendish International

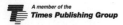
A member of the
Times Publishing Group

Other Marshall Cavendish Offices:
Marshall Cavendish Corporation. 99 White Plains Road, Tarrytown NY 10591-9001,
USA • Marshall Cavendish International (Thailand) Co Ltd. 253 Asoke, 12th Floor,
Sukhumvit 21 Road, Klongtoey Nua, Wattana, Bangkok 10110, Thailand • Marshall
Cavendish (Malaysia) Sdn Bhd, Times Subang, Lot 46, Subang Hi-Tech Industrial
Park, Batu Tiga, 40000 Shah Alam, Selangor Darul Ehsan, Malaysia

Marshall Cavendish is a registered trademark of Times Publishing Limited

National Library Board, Singapore Cataloguing-in-Publication Data
Names: Shaw, Peter, 1949–
Title: 100 Great Leading Through Frustration Ideas / Dr Peter Shaw.
Description: Singapore : Marshall Cavendish Business, [2019]
Identifiers: OCN 1083511603 | ISBN 978-981-4841-47-4
Subjects: LCSH: Problem solving. | Psychology, Industrial.
Classification: DDC 658.403–dc23

Cover image by Pressfoto/Freepik.com

Printed in Singapore

Dedicated to all those who have lived through
frustration and retained the capacity
to laugh at themselves

TITLES IN THE 100 **GREAT IDEAS** SERIES

CONTENTS

Section D: Act

Section E: Observe

Section F: Reframe

Section G: Internal frustrations

Section H: Frustrations caused by others

Section I: Handling frustrations with specific people

Section J: Handling frustrations with policies and processes

Section K: Leading through frustrations caused by specific prompts

Section L: Keeping cool through frustration

ACKNOWLEDGEMENTS

I HAVE HAD the privilege of working closely with many leaders and teams who have lead through frustrating circumstances. Often frustrations are externally generated, but sometimes they result from internal wrestling. I have observed many instances where frustration has led to creative and purposeful action. On other occasions frustration has taken time to address and move through. I have learnt so much from the people I have worked with who have been leading through frustrations and have tried to distil some of that learning into this book.

My thanks go to colleagues at Praesta Partners who have been sources of practical ideas and have always been willing to challenge my thinking. In particular I want to thank Paul Gray, Hilary Douglas, Louise Shepherd and Una O'Brien for their sound advice and perspective.

I am grateful to Duncan Selbie for writing the foreword to this book. Duncan is an outstanding leader who has been an inspiration to many developing leaders. He and I have had many conversations reflecting on how best a leader draws out capabilities and enables frustration to be turned into fruitful pushing of boundaries.

Melvin Neo at Marshall Cavendish has been an excellent sponsor for this series. He has always been supportive about my developing ideas for the series. Mike Spilling has been an admirable copy editor of the text. Janine Gamilla has provided lots of practical support.

Jackie Tookey has typed the manuscript with her usual care and efficiency. Tracy Easthope has managed my diary to enable me to have the space to write. Together, Jackie and Tracy have been a wonderful support team to whom I owe a great deal. Anthony Hopkins and

Jo Gavin have provided excellent support in enabling me to do my coaching work at Praesta Partners.

My younger son, Colin, helped me think through the structure for this book. He and I worked out the suggested five steps for leading through frustration during a delightful conversation. Conversations with my elder son, Graham, and my daughter, Ruth, always provide insights into what makes people tick and how best to respond and influence, whatever the encircling frustrations. I am very grateful to Frances, my wife, for her encouragement and practical support throughout this project.

FOREWORD

FRUSTRATION IS PART of leadership. Frustration leads to action and progress. As a leader, you need to face into frustration and not ignore it. Frustration needs to be channelled and not feared. Frustration can lead to fabulous consequences when the cause of the frustration is addressed and necessary action taken.

When you feel frustrated, believe in yourself. When you have thought through your approach, stay with it and do not be diverted by the frustrations of others. Keep a focus on doing the right thing, having carefully considered the perspectives of those around you. Walk knowingly into difficult conversations and do not hide from them. The causes of frustration sometimes have to be named and openly tackled.

Sometimes you have to live with ambiguity, which means an underlying level of frustration continues. You have to stay with it in imperfect circumstances, while being clear in your own mind what you believe are the right next steps. You stop yourself feeling resentful if others seem to be pushing in an unhelpful direction or are being seemingly duplicitous in their approach. You act as a result of clear thinking rather than responding to frustration, recognising that frustration in you unleashes insight and action.

When you feel frustrated with yourself, remember to forgive yourself. Have in your head a forgiveness committee. You share with the committee why you took your chosen action. You did what you thought was the right thing. The forgiveness committee always listens and allows you to explain what you have learnt and how you are going to move on.

At moments of frustration, it helps to stand aside, if only for a brief moment. You briefly review the evidence. You know what are the key facts and principles. You remember what are the underlying values that are fundamental to you.

You appoint people who are able to respond to frustration and manage their own frustrations. You develop them and invest in them. Seek to understand what causes frustration in those who work for you and enable them to convert that frustration into positive action rather than destructive angst.

Frustrated people have energy which when unleashed can have a profound effect for good. They need to be engaged and not ignored, embraced and not cast aside. See dialogue with frustrated people as helping you to sharpen your thinking and approach. Your engagement with them may lead to unexpected alliances based on mutual respect.

In 22 years in chief executive roles across the health world, I have known frustrations of many different shapes and sizes. I commend this book by Peter Shaw as a treasure trove of ideas for leading through frustration. He sets out a very clear framework of (1) understand, (2) plan, (3) act, (4) observe and (5) reframe. He provides insights into handling internal frustrations and those caused by people, policies and circumstances, with a focus on how to keep your cool living through myriad frustrations.

Peter and I have worked together for approaching 10 years, meeting regularly for a 7 a.m. breakfast, when we always have engaging and cheerful conversations. As you read this book, imagine that you are having breakfast with Peter, smiling about your frustrations as a leader and engaging with ways of moving forward, rather than being stuck in the past or the present.

Duncan Selbie
Chief Executive
Public Health England

INTRODUCTION

THE TITLE "LEADING THROUGH FRUSTRATION" is deliberately multi-layered. Sometimes we are leading through our own frustrations, sometimes we are leading other people through theirs. This book is intended to provide a framework for leading yourself and others through frustration. It sets out a five-point plan with the following steps:

1. Understand
2. Plan
3. Act
4. Observe
5. Reframe

Frustrations keep changing and our capacity to handle frustration keeps evolving. We can never stand still for long. The book seeks to enable the reader to address their frustrations in a fresh and constructive way. Realism is key in addressing frustrations, alongside a belief that through frustration you learn and can make discoveries about yourself and others. Frustrations can lead to breakthroughs and new beginnings when handled carefully.

This book complements the other volumes in the '100 Great Ideas' series, which explore personal impact, coaching, team effectiveness, building success, leading well and handling rapid change. As you dip into individual chapters, I hope that ideas will stay with you and enable you to address frustrations in a fresh and helpful way. The first five chapters summarise the themes underpinning the whole book.

I trust the book will provide a useful framework and practical ideas that will enable you to lead well through frustration and be on a continuous journey of developing the way you lead yourself and others through demanding situations. I hope the book will enable you to develop effective ways to understand, plan, act, observe and reframe your frustrations. The hypothetical examples in the book might provide useful prompts that catch your imagination about what is possible.

As we lead through frustrations, we develop new insights and resilience, which help us stand back in the face of challenges and uncertainties.

Canon Professor Peter Shaw CB PhD DCL(Hon)
Godalming, England
peter.shaw@praesta.com

SECTION A
A FIVE-POINT PLAN FOR LEADING THROUGH FRUSTRATION

UNDERSTAND

WE NEED TO TAKE TIME to understand rather than rush to act.

The idea

Why might we be feeling frustrated? What has happened that has created a climate of frustration? Why is there an undercurrent of frustration that is sapping the energy and resolve of a team? Why is my first reaction frustration when I think about my work?

When frustration begins to eat us up, or detrimentally affect the way individuals or a team operates, the first step is to seek to understand what is going on. There may be obvious reasons for the frustration that everyone involved recognises. There might be a complex set of interactions that cause frustration to some and not to others.

How best can we stand back and observe and understand a situation rather than becoming totally immersed in it or overwhelmed by it? A starting point is to seek to understand the underlying reasons for our own frustration, alongside the cause of frustration in others. It is helpful to reflect on how we have handled frustrations in the past and what we have learnt from those experiences: perhaps we handle frustrations very differently now compared to the past.

It can be relevant to appreciate what aspects of your personality magnify the frustration effect. Life experience may have taught you how best to handle situations where your personal character or vulnerabilities mean that frustration can quickly escalate. Perhaps there is a risk of you enjoying being frustrated sometimes, if that allows you to feel a victim or elicits the sympathy you think you deserve.

Barbara could feel indignant with frustration. Sometimes she felt that no one took her seriously. She deliberately delegated significant responsibilities to others but became inwardly frustrated if they did not act precisely in the way she had hoped. Barbara's family teased her that she liked to be in control; she recognised this characteristic in herself.

In the past, Barbara had become frustrated if colleagues did not follow her instructions precisely. She had trained herself to be much less expectant that they would do exactly as she wanted. She had learnt how to stand back from this initial frustrated reaction. There had been moments when she had relished her own frustration when others made decisions she did not agree with. Over time she had become better at understanding her own frustrations and explained to herself what was creating this frustration.

In practice

- Be as dispassionate as possible in identifying the underlying reasons for your frustrations.

- Recognise when you can be the cause of frustration in others through the way you act.

- Build on learning from how you have handled frustrations in the past.

- Be honest to yourself about the aspects of your personality that tend to exacerbate feeling being frustrated.

- Acknowledge when there is a risk of wallowing in your own frustration.

2 PLAN

PUTTING TOGETHER A PLAN is rarely wasted, although it might need to be regularly adapted.

The idea

When we feel the victim of our own frustrations or we see others gripped by frustration, we need to feel that we can move on from being captive to frustration. Once we understand the reasons for our frustration, there is the prospect of putting together a plan to address those frustrations. The starting point is discriminating between the frustrations we can do something about and those that are outside our control.

When we are at risk of feeling overwhelmed by frustrations it can help to think through which frustrations need to be addressed first. They may appear of equal difficulty, but they can normally be ranked in some order. Which frustration do we need to address first in order to progress in handling other frustrations? Sometimes we need to address our own frustrations first before we can satisfactorily tackle others' frustrations. Sometimes progress has to be made addressing the frustrations of our staff or partner groups before there is any prospect of addressing our own frustrations.

A starting point in planning to address frustrations involves recognising when shared frustrations can lead to unhelpful groupthink or to magnifying a relatively minor problem into an apparent crisis. Effective planning involves a combination of taking time to interrogate frustrations in order to put them into perspective, and then to decide on steps needed to address sequentially particular frustrations. There is always a risk of jumping from understanding to acting, with the consequence of well-meaning but uncoordinated actions that may succeed only in replacing one frustration with another.

Barbara used to get very frustrated by her inability to plan ahead. This frustration with herself and her colleagues seemed to grip her and disable her thinking. Having understood more about what caused her frustration, Barbara recognised that she needed to take some small steps to address those frustrations. She had to de-escalate the risk of calamity in her mind. Planning a few practical steps to ease her frustrations did not come easily to her, but she knew she had to put a convincing plan in place that would feel robust enough to move forward. Barbara recognised that she needed an approach to creating a plan, and then a means of standing back to assess what would enable that plan to be effective.

In practice

- Be deliberate in differentiating between frustrations you can do something about and those outside your control.

- Differentiate between those frustrations that need to be addressed first and those that can wait.

- Be mindful whether your planning needs to take account of the risk of unhelpful groupthink.

- Decide on the necessary sequence of steps to address particular frustrations.

- Plan to take time out to assess frustrations and your progress in addressing them.

3 ACT

LEADING THROUGH FRUSTRATION will require action that is focused and is not divided between too many fronts at the same time.

The idea

When we feel burdened by frustration, we can feel a victim of circumstance and unable to take meaningful actions to address complicated situations. There might be surges of energy and an impulse to act to demonstrate that we have addressed our frustration. When we see the possibility of action, there is a danger that we act in haste and regret at leisure. Action that is sustainable needs to be deliberate, focused and measured. Action that is part of a plan is more likely to combine effectively with other actions rather than being a random initiative.

Sustainable action can start from recognising when frustration can release energy that leads to positive, sustained change. Action can flow when we accept that some frustrations have to be lived with and involve making the best of a sub-optimal situation. The overwhelming requirement is to be in the right frame of mind prior to taking action. When clear understanding has led to a thought-through plan and a positive frame of mind, there is a reasonable prospect that you will have the fortitude and resilience to move through your frustration into a state where there is a clearer equilibrium.

An action is far more likely to be sustained when you log the progress made and recognise what is likely to work well or less well. When you have supporters and allies, your ability to act effectively through frustration will be greatly enhanced.

Barbara felt the frustration about the apparent complacency of some colleagues building up in her mind so that she was almost demonising them. She knew she had to understand what was happening both to her colleagues and herself. She could see in her mind's eye a plan that would build a stronger sense of shared endeavour. She had to decide whether to let her frustration continue to fuel indifference towards her colleagues, or whether she could turn that frustration into decisive steps.

Barbara recognised that she had to take the initiative to build momentum for a way forward that would benefit all the different groups in the organisation. But she had to get into a frame of mind where she believed the attitudes of her colleagues could be changed, with their curiosity stimulated about finding new solutions to vexatious problems.

In practice

- Allow your frustration to lead to concerted action.

- Be deliberate in how you live with frustrations that are not going to go away.

- Be conscious about steering yourself into the right frame of mind so that you act in constructive and not negative ways.

- Log progress made and keep building on successful action.

- Act in consort with your allies and supporters.

4 OBSERVE

WE NEED TO KEEP observing ourselves as others see us and ensure
we see different situations through a variety of lenses.

The idea

Young children observe what their parents do and mirror that
behaviour. The more we observe others and ourselves, the more
discerning we will become in how we handle frustrations. When we
observe others handling frustrations well, we can deliberately mirror
their approaches. When we see them handling frustrations sub-
optimally, we can be reminded how our approach can detrimentally
affect others.

As we observe ourselves, we can be mindful of the difference between
constructive frustration that leads to positive and decisive action, in
contrast to resentment that saps energy and undermines our beliefs
about the right way forward and the values that guide us. Observing
how you interact with others will offer you a perspective about when
you might be at risk of projecting your frustrations onto others.

It helps to identify the pattern of your reactions to frustration.
Sometimes your reactions can be self-destructive. On other occasions
you may be impressed by your own reactions, which combine
acceptance of the inevitable with a deliberate resolve to help change
direction in a constructive way.

Observing ourselves is not about self-indulgence. It involves being
deliberate in seeing how we react in different situations, and how
others react to us. It involves recognising when we can provoke

frustrations in others and blow issues out of proportion. It involves the capacity to be fully involved as a player in a fast-moving context, and yet detached enough to recognise what is happening and not overwhelmed by the risks or overawed by the personalities.

Barbara knew she needed to keep a careful eye on her own emotions. Her frustration could sometimes turn into constructive action, but on other occasions it led to resentment. She sometimes could not predict where her frustration would lead her. She used to observe with amusement when frustration turned into constructive next steps and when she became heated with indignation.

Barbara recognised that she needed to see herself as others saw her, so that she was conscious of how her frustrations could project onto others. Sometimes she wanted others to see her frustration because she sought to elicit a response from them. On other occasions she wanted to ensure that others could not observe her frustration, because she recognised that it was hers to deal with and not something that she should let contaminate her relationship with others.

In practice

- Recognise how others handle similar frustrations to yours.

- Watch how the way you handle frustration affects others.

- Be conscious of the fine line between constructive frustration and resentment.

- Be mindful if you appear to project your frustrations onto others.

- Observe the pattern of your reactions to frustration and use that to refine your own self-understanding.

5 REFRAME

A KEY TO HANDLING frustration is to reframe the different elements of the frustration you experience so that you are drawing out the positive and not being destroyed by the negative.

The idea

Darkness can be described as bleak, hopeless and never-ending. Darkness can also be described as the interval before the dawn. All reality can be viewed through a variety of lenses. We can see frustration as inevitable and leading to destructive consequences. On the other hand, we can believe that good can come out of any situation. We can believe that if we look dispassionately at any frustration, there is the possibility of seeing a way forward. We can try to block out interfering noises that get in the way of us seeing the possibilities that can flow from apparent frustrations. We can reframe a small step forward as a significant move in the right direction. We can see a setback as part of a continuous learning process that is never-ending.

This is not an encouragement to reframe in a way that denies underlying truth or blocks out the inevitable. We can see the future as involving inevitable death. We can also see the future as being full of interesting conversations, with lots of opportunities to shape a worthwhile future for ourselves and others.

At the heart of handling frustration is deciding how we frame our attitude to a particular situation. We are able to choose each day what is our attitude to a frustration. When we receive a difficult prognosis, we can either be filled with gloom or begin to think through how we are going to use our time and energy to best effect. We can be devastated with frustration about missed opportunities, or we can reframe our way of thinking to be thankful for a full life and glad of opportunities that still exist to learn, engage and encourage.

Barbara recognised that she needed to reframe her current view about her work situation. She could choose to be gloomy about what was going wrong, or she could believe that she was learning a huge amount about herself and her colleagues. She had to decide the attitude she brought to her current situation. Was she continually going to focus on the problems, or was she going to develop possibilities that the frustrations were opening up? She could describe herself as on a relentless conveyor belt of frustrations or on a never-ending journey of continuous learning. Barbara knew the attitude of mind that would keep her cheerful and enjoyable to be with.

In practice

- Look for the good that can flow out of any situation.

- Identify clearly issues causing you and others frustration.

- Be deliberate in blocking out interfering noises in your head.

- Believe that even a small step forward is a major advance.

- Enjoy never-ending learning.

- Always choose to reframe to see opportunities ahead rather than possibilities missed.

SECTION B
UNDERSTAND

WHAT ARE THE REASONS FOR YOUR FRUSTRATION?

6

THE MORE YOU UNDERSTAND the reasons for your frustration, the greater the likelihood you can deal with that frustration effectively.

The idea

Our frustrations come from many different sources. The causes might be deep-seated or a consequence of recent events. A frustration might feel acute because we are tired, irritated or disappointed. We might handle a reverse well on one day, while on other occasions we might become annoyed and frustrated. Sometimes situations or comments flick the frustration button while on other occasions we take events in our stride.

When we begin to feel frustrated by an event or an individual, it is worth standing back, at least metaphorically if not physically, in order to seek to understand the reasons for that frustration. What has triggered it on this occasion? What is the underlying unresolved issue that might have caused this frustration to surface? Is this a frustration that is likely to pass quickly, or is it a deep-seated frustration that is likely to hang around for a few days if it is not addressed?

When we are in the grip of a frustration, it is difficult to be released from it. We can feel captive to our emotions and unable to break out of that sense of annoyance as we keep wrestling with a particular issue. The more we can stand back and articulate to ourselves why we are feeling frustrated by a particular situation or individual, the greater the likelihood of our being able to contain that frustration and stop it contaminating the rest of our thinking. The more objective we can be in recognising the reasons for our frustration, the greater the likelihood that we can limit the emotional energy wasted on holding this frustration at bay.

Jane was a senior partner in a medical practice. Life felt full of frustrations: she saw her colleagues, the patients and the Department of Health all being equally responsible for her frustration. Her patients often ignored what she said. Her colleagues did not appear to listen to her. The Department of Health did not seem to have any appreciation of the pressures on doctors.

Jane recognised that after a long week she needed time to process her feelings and to understand why she felt so frustrated. What were the particular reasons why the decisions of others had so annoyed her? She recognised there had been a combination of circumstances, with some individuals triggering feelings of resentment. Once Jane began to understand the reasons for her frustration, she felt she could begin to move on and even look forward to the next week.

In practice

- Seek to differentiate between the apparent reasons for your frustration and the underlying causes.

- Identify the three key reasons for your feeling of frustration.

- When you feel your emotions are getting the better of you, go deeper in exploring the underlying causes of the frustration.

- Seek to move into a different mental space to identify as objectively as you can the triggers for your frustration.

WHEN ARE YOU THE CAUSE OF FRUSTRATION IN OTHERS?

IT IS HELPFUL TO UNDERSTAND how you can be the cause of frustration in others.

The idea

Sometimes we are deliberate in causing frustration in other people. We ask them to take on tasks that they might not wish to do. We expect timetables to be met that seem to them to be ambitious. We can create expectations that can seem daunting. We are demanding of other people because of the pressures on us or because we judge that setting clear expectations will bring out the best in them.

Sometimes we can be the cause of frustration in others without realising it. We might not have appreciated how a particular request or expectation is going to be perceived. We may observe a thin smile or a slightly furrowed brow without realising the effect we have had on the recipient of that request or comment. If we do not receive feedback about how we are causing frustration in others, we can continue with the same pattern of behaviour for an extended period without being aware of our impact.

When you set out an expectation for others or make specific requests, it can be helpful to reflect on how you would feel if the same request was placed on you. It is worth thinking about how individuals have responded to your expectations and requests in the past. Feedback from different observers can be helpful in drawing attention to when you have been the cause of frustration in others and what have been the consequences of that frustration, for good or ill.

As senior partner, Jane recognised that it was her role to set out clear expectations about the approach of the doctors to their work. Following consultation with her colleagues, it was her responsibility to be explicit about the expectations of the quality of the doctors' work and the way they interacted with patients. Jane recognised that part of her job was to work with her colleagues to ensure that professional expectations were met, and accepted that this would cause frustration on some occasions for her colleagues. She recognised that she needed to be deliberate in setting expectations and following those expectations through.

Jane recognised that she could, on some occasions, appear a bit brusque. When she was tired or busy, her tone could come across as a shade harsh. Jane knew that when she was feeling tired she had to be deliberate in the words she chose and the tone of her voice. She did not want to cause frustration in others inadvertently because of her manner or tone of voice.

In practice

- Recognise what causes frustration in the people you work with.

- Be deliberate in choosing when you want to be the cause of frustration in others.

- Be mindful of when you can inadvertently cause frustration in others through your tone of voice or how you frame requests.

- Beware if your mindset is never to want to cause frustration in others.

HOW BEST HAVE YOU HANDLED FRUSTRATION IN THE PAST?

RECOGNISING HOW YOU HANDLED frustrations effectively in the past provides helpful data about how you can best handle them in the future.

The idea

We have all developed techniques for handling frustrations. Some of those approaches may be effective, while others might be counter-productive. Our approaches might be heavily engrained in the way we respond to particular stimuli. Sometimes we will respond in a constructive way, which flows from understanding the cause of the frustration and identifying practical steps we can take to move forward. But we might be equally conscious of occasions when we have responded to frustrations in a self-destructive way.

When a frustration arises, it can be worth reflecting on how you handled a similar challenge well in the past. What helped you view the situation as objectively as possible? What did you learn from that situation which you might apply in similar situations going forward? No two frustrations are exactly the same but there is always learning that flows from reflecting on how you handled past frustrations.

It is worth distinguishing between how you handled frustrating situations when the expectation or request was within the bounds of reasonableness, and your response to expectations that were completely unreasonable. A further category might be your response to frustrations that just appear as annoyances: you might have woken up one morning feeling frustrated without being able to identify the cause. Sometimes you might have addressed a frustration directly, and on other occasions your approach might have been to deliberately fill your mind with other thoughts to seek to displace the frustration.

Jane recognised that one of her colleagues was consistently likely to frustrate her because of his offhand manner. Jane knew that she became most irritated when caught unawares by a comment from this colleague. Jane recognised that she had to take a deep breath and not respond instantly when this individual was causing her frustration.

When progress was slow in taking forward necessary changes within the medical practice, Jane knew she had to be deliberate in writing down what she thought were the key reasons for the limited progress, and then with her colleagues address each of these individual concerns in a deliberate and measured way.

In practice

- Recall occasions when a systematic approach to addressing frustration has been successful in identifying the causes.

- Remember when you have broken down into a sequence of small steps how you have handled your own frustrations.

- Try to distinguish between your handling of reasonable expectations from others and expectations or requests that have been unreasonable.

- Reinforce in your mind how you have effectively handled frustrations that have caused you the greatest emotional aggravation.

WHAT ASPECTS OF YOUR PERSONALITY MAGNIFY THE FRUSTRATION EFFECT?

BEING SELF-AWARE ABOUT HOW your personality can magnify the frustration effect can provide valuable insights into how to handle frustrations going forward.

The idea

The distinctiveness of our personality is what differentiates us as people. We are each unique and bring our own particular approach. Inevitably our personality will appeal to some and be less attractive to others. Our personality can cause frustration for others, which we might be oblivious to; hence it is important to understand from colleagues and friends how our personality can create frustrations. Your personality can also be a source of considerable frustration to yourself.

If our natural approach is to need time to reflect on issues before we are ready to reach a view, then an expectation that we make quick decisions can cause uncomfortable frustration. If we are at our best when we are able to talk issues through with others, we may feel stymied if confidentiality requirements mean that we can't seek the advice of other people.

If our natural preference is to plan ahead, we can be frustrated by colleagues who like to operate at speed and at the last minute. If our preference is to look at the bigger picture, we can be frustrated by those who want to begin with the detail. What can be hugely helpful is understanding the preferences of both yourself and colleagues so that you recognise when you are most likely to rub up against each other and cause frustration.

When you are feeling frustrated, questioning which aspects of your personality are magnifying the frustration effect can be helpful. Simply identifying three reasons why your personality is magnifying your emotional reaction to a situation can be helpful in diminishing the sense of frustration.

Jane recognised that she got annoyed if colleagues were preoccupied with what she regarded as small details. When the group of doctors met together, Jane's preference was to focus on strategic, longer-term questions about the direction the practice was taking. She knew that some individuals would want to examine detailed concerns first. When Jane became a senior partner, this difference of approach caused her considerable frustration. After a while she recognised that she had to work with the grain of all the different personalities.

Jane's colleagues needed time in these meetings to address detailed issues before they would be ready to think constructively about longer-term questions. Jane accepted that she could not fight this pattern and needed to conduct meetings in a way that took account of the personal characteristics of her different colleagues. Jane had to manage her own sense of irritation when her colleagues were overly concerned about details; but she also recognised that her preference for dealing with the longer-term issues was the reason why she had been appointed as Senior Partner and why her judgement was trusted by her colleagues.

In practice

- When are your personal preferences your greatest asset or your biggest liability?

- When might aspects of your personality be a cause of frustration to others?

- What is it about your personality that causes most frustration in your colleagues?

- How best do you handle your own counter-productive personal preferences that stop you operating at your best?

WHEN IS THERE A RISK OF YOU ENJOYING BEING FRUSTRATED?

THERE IS A RISK that we indulge in being frustrated and seeing ourselves as a victim.

The idea

There are moments when we might quite enjoy being frustrated. We can feel hard done by and a victim. We can construct in our mind reasons for our frustration, depicting others as the villain and us as the hero. We can enjoy the self-worth that comes from standing up to the frustration caused by others. We can construct a scenario whereby we take pride in our resilience and are amazed by our own fortitude and resolve.

Frustration becomes a frame of mind that we can even relish or wallow in. Enjoying frustration can lead us to believe we are always right, with everyone else perceived as irrelevant and destructive. When we reach the stage of enjoying being frustrated, we need to be mindful of the danger signs and conscious of when we might be demonising others and building up a false sense of our own virtues.

On the other hand, it is worth remembering that frustration can have huge positive effects. There will have been moments for all of us when frustration has led to a positive resolve to make a difference. In retrospect, we can see those times of frustration as defining moments that have enabled us to take a forward step or to develop a clear strategy.

The sense of frustration might not of itself have been enjoyable, but addressing the frustration may have created its own sense of satisfaction as you developed an approach that moved you out of frustration and toward a constructive way forward. There might have been a defining moment where you began to see practical next steps clearly ahead.

Jane used to get frustrated by some of her patients who did not respect the time constraints that she was operating under. This frustration led to her feeling self-righteous about her calling as a doctor. She began to say to herself, 'How dare people waste my precious time?' She quite enjoyed this sense of frustration, but demonising her patients did not help her treat them well. Jane developed techniques to enable some lugubrious patients to get to the point more quickly. She sought to turn her frustration into a sense of satisfaction by getting some of her talkative patients to address the key issues more directly.

In practice

- When have you been at risk of enjoying being frustrated and how was that apparent?

- How much of your self-worth is tied up in feeling virtuous when others are frustrating you?

- When have moments of frustration led to breakthroughs, followed by moments of enjoyment as you have seen a way forward?

SECTION C
PLAN

DISCRIMINATE BETWEEN THE FRUSTRATIONS YOU CAN DO SOMETHING ABOUT AND THOSE OUTSIDE OF YOUR CONTROL

THERE ARE SOME FRUSTRATIONS you can do something about. Others you have to live with. What matters is how you manage frustrations that are outside your control.

The idea

You may feel you have limited resources in order to deliver what is expected of you. You may have sought to get additional resources but have been told it is not realistic at this stage. For the immediate future the resources you have available are outside your control and there is little point in allowing yourself to be overwhelmed by frustration about this. You might have some influence over the expectations of what can be delivered if you can formulate a clear case about relative priorities and impact. You may have some control about the sequencing of next steps and how you deploy the resources available to you. You do have some influence over your attitude of mind and can choose how much you allow yourself to be frustrated or show your frustration.

You might be working in partnership with a colleague who frustrates you. This colleague is in post for the foreseeable future so it is outside your control to determine whether this person stays or goes; but you do have a choice about how you work with this colleague and how you handle your own frustrations when seeking to bring different approaches.

As a civil servant you might be frustrated by the approach of a particular Minister; but they are an appointee of a democratically elected government and you have to live with the frustration that flows from their approach. You can address your own frustration by seeking to understand what is driving the Minister to make decisions and act in a particular way.

Tom was initially excited about working for a new Minister. Tom had enjoyed a close working relationship with the previous Minister as his private secretary and was confident that he would be able to work effectively with any new Minister, but the new Minister was preoccupied with political considerations and did not seem very interested in the work of the Department. The Minister was not good at reading his briefs and was slow in handling submissions and making decisions. Tom became increasingly frustrated with what he regarded as the unhelpful and almost irresponsible behaviour of his Minister.

Tom took the advice of an experienced mentor who encouraged him to accept that each Minister has their own way of doing things. It was important that a Minister kept in touch with their political roots. It was for Tom to find a way of working with the new Minister and not expect the new Minister to act in the same way as his predecessor. It was Tom's job to find ways of ensuring that submissions to the Minister were presented in the most effective way so that decisions were made.

In practice

- Recognise that some causes of frustration are completely outside of your control.

- Recognise the elements that you can influence that will help reduce your frustration.

- Accept that you have choices in the way you allow yourself to be frustrated by the actions and approaches of others.

- Take satisfaction about where you can influence others in a way that reduces shared frustrations.

THINK THROUGH WHICH FRUSTRATIONS NEED TO BE ADDRESSED FIRST

FRUSTRATION EASILY OVERWHELMS US. Being systematic in deciding which frustration is dealt with first can help us make progress and feel that we are making progress.

The idea

Frustrations can easily overwhelm us. When we dwell on one frustration, our mind can jump to another frustration and we compound one frustration on top of another. We can soon end up in a spiral of despondency, with each frustration becoming increasingly oppressive.

It can be helpful to ask yourself which frustration needs to be addressed first, and what aspect of that frustration needs to be tackled as a first step. Breaking down a frustration into small component steps can help a difficult situation feel more manageable. If the desired steps are small and realistic, we are more likely to make progress. If the frustration is about your attitude of mind, the next step might be to think about what you need to accept as inevitable and what is within the bounds of practicality.

It can help to decide that you are going to think through your next steps in addressing one frustration today and park for later thinking through your approach to a different frustration. If there is a confusion of both work and personal frustrations in your mind, it can help to say to yourself that you are going to focus on the work frustration in work time and leave the personal frustration to a non-work time.

You might conclude that the best way of working through a particular frustration is while doing physical exercise. Or you might conclude that the best way of addressing a particular frustration is to talk it through with a trusted colleague or friend—the next step being to fix a time for a coffee with that friend or colleague.

After a week working for his new Minister, Tom recognised that he needed to stop feeling overwhelmed with frustration. He accepted that he needed to get over his own grief about the previous Minister moving on. Departmental officials were particularly concerned about the lack of decisions being taken by the Minister on some key submissions. Tom recognised that his key priority was to help the Minister get to a point where he could make decisions on time-sensitive issues. The operational needs of the Department's business required decisions from the Minister. The frustration about the indecision of the Minister was the key frustration to be addressed. Tom's personal preferences about how to work with a new Minister were secondary, albeit important to Tom. He had to find a way forward that worked well for the Minister.

In practice

- Which frustration, if not tackled, will detrimentally affect the work of your organisation?

- Which frustrations are about your emotions and, therefore, secondary to delivering the work of the organisation?

- As you identify the three frustrations that need to be addressed first, can you talk through this prioritisation with trusted others?

- Is there a coherence between the frustrations which you would like to tackle first and the relative importance of these frustrations?

- How best do you break down into achievable steps the frustration you are going to tackle first?

RECOGNISE WHEN SHARED FRUSTRATION IS LEADING TO UNHELPFUL GROUPTHINK

SHARED FRUSTRATION CAN easily boil over into attitudes and actions that can be destructive.

The idea

A shared frustration can quickly build up into a sense of exasperation or defeatism. It can boil over into aggressive words and actions. Quite rapidly a few fairly innocent expressions of concern can build up into a heated sense of indignation.

Industrial relations are full of examples where management has built up a picture of an unhelpful workforce, while at the same time the unions have demonised management. The groupthink on both sides has turned industrial relations into a battlefield.

The rapid rise in the use of social media has demonstrated how quickly groupthink can create excessive emotions and lead to the demonising of individuals who have taken decisions for perfectly logical reasons.

The risk of groupthink is reduced if a team includes people with a range of different approaches. It is key for any group to be looking for external perspectives and seeking feedback on how their attitude and approaches are expressed. It is good to question on a regular basis if a group is at risk of counter-productive groupthink. This reinforces the importance of welcoming external scrutiny and not feeling that scrutiny is a threat.

A group acting together with strong resolve and lots of mutual support is a powerful agent for change. A unified group with a clear, shared purpose enables each member to deliver more than they could individually. But groupthink that is not independently assessed can result in railroading through ambitions without regard to changing circumstances and the views of affected individuals. Group action can be very powerful, while groupthink can be highly dangerous.

Tom enjoyed working with colleagues in the ministerial private office. In the first couple of weeks with the new Minister, there was a shared frustration. The plus was that the private office team bonded together and was supportive of each other. The minus was that frustrations with the new Minister tended to be talked up, with the private office team becoming increasingly critical of their new Minister and longing for their previous Minister.

After a good conversation with his mentor, Tom began to recognise the risk of groupthink in the private office. He brought together the private office team and talked through how they were going to respond in a more constructive way to the preferences of the new Minister. They needed to move on from their shared grief and frustration into a more positive frame of mind. They needed to act together as a cohesive, forward-looking group and not be looking backwards to better days.

In practice

- What is the difference between a committed group's focus on shared outcomes, and a groupthink that distorts reality?

- When have you observed groupthink being myopic and avoiding harsh reality?

- How best do you ensure that groupthink does not develop to distort reality?

- When can groupthink mean that partnerships with other key groups or players are put at risk?

DECIDE ON THE STEPS TO ADDRESS PARTICULAR FRUSTRATIONS

BE DELIBERATE IN DECIDING on the steps needed to address particular frustrations. Some of the steps will be about attitudes and others will be about actions.

The idea

When I am on a long-distance walk in the summer, I am equipped with a sun hat and sun cream. Whatever the time of year, I have waterproofs in the rucksack. I know the steps I will take if the sun beats down or the rain is torrential. If there is a long climb ahead, I know the frame of mind I need as I trudge up the steep hillside or mountain pass. I may be frustrated by my slow progress, but I hold in my mind the view from the summit and that sense of achievement as I reach my goal.

We can equip ourselves to address practical frustrations. We have our plan B if a timetable is not met. We have our contingent arrangements to address known risks. Equally important are the attitudes of mind we deploy if a frustrating situation is likely to continue for a while. As you plan how to handle a particular frustration, it is worth thinking through in some detail the particular actions you want to take and the attitudes of mind you want to bring.

Progress is dependent on that combination of attitude and action. They go in tandem and need to be adaptable. The initial attitude may need to be one of step-by-step determination, reinforced by the recognition that there will be a sense of satisfaction as progress is made. The determined step-by-step action may need to be unrelenting for a period, with the knowledge that progress leads to renewed momentum.

Tom was deliberate with his private office team in working through both the actions they needed to take with the new Minister to ensure progress was made, and the attitudes that were necessary to ensure a rapport was built up with the new Minister. They needed to be clear what mattered most to the Minister about the service provided by the private office. Tom recognised that there needed to be a much stronger sense of warmth and personal engagement with the new Minister.

After a couple of weeks the Minister was becoming more settled in his role and more willing to listen with an open mind to officials. Tom began to see some positive qualities in the new Minister; there were touches of humour in their conversations. Tom recognised in the new Minister insights that flowed from conversations with constituents. Tom began to see and appreciate the political perspective and understanding that the Minister brought. They were beginning to make progress. Tom was relieved that they had been working through their frustrations as a private office and not giving up on serving the new Minister well.

In practice

- In dealing with a particular frustration, what is the right balance between the actions you need to take and the attitude you need to bring?

- How best do you decide on your next steps in addressing a particular frustration in a way that brings key people with you?

- How best do you prepare yourself for the long haul when you know you are going to have to live with a frustration for a period before seeing evidence of progress?

- How will you mark the progress you have made towards addressing a particular frustration?

TAKE TIME OUT TO PUT FRUSTRATIONS INTO PERSPECTIVE

WE EACH NEED OUR own method of putting our frustrations into perspective and applying that method on a regular basis.

The idea

I put my frustrations into perspective when I go on long walks. For some, the physical exertion of running, cycling or swimming can have the same beneficial effect. For others, it is listening to music, reading a book or talking with the children in their lives. Each of us will have a method of putting frustrations into perspective. Some of these methods will be inherently healthy, while others may be destructive. An over-dependence on eating, drinking and surfing the web might be a means of handling our frustrations, but it won't help put them into perspective.

Talking with a trusted mentor or coach is never wasted time. Constructive, forward-looking conversation with an independent person can help us crystallise next steps and develop a confident and measured way forward.

Time out to put frustrations into perspective in the heat of the moment might include a five-minute break or a 15-minute walk around the block. We are rarely in a situation where it is impossible to take a brief time out to reflect about an issue from a different angle. Time out to reflect is not an indulgence: it is a necessary part of survival and adaptation to changing circumstances. Part of putting frustrations into perspective is recognising which ones are of most significance and which are preoccupying you.

It can be helpful to ask yourself, which frustrations have I got completely out of proportion and which do I need to leave behind? Amputating a frustration is best done when you are away from a particular situation and able to look at future possibilities in a dispassionate way. Most frustrations are far less significant than they appear to be in the dead of night.

Tom recognised that he needed to get his frustrations with his new Minister into proportion before he could help his team do the same thing. For Tom, the approach that worked was a combination of talking with his mentor and going for a brisk cycle ride on Saturday morning. Tom decided that the best way of handling the team was to have a session on a Friday in which they openly shared their frustrations about working with the Minister. Tom then guided them to reflect on what were some of the advantages of the new Minister and how best they could work with him going forward.

Tom invited the team members to talk through how best they moved on from their frustration, recognising the reality of the new situation. Tom talked with the team about building on their professionalism to ensure that they provided the best possible service to the new Minister, which meant building a strong rapport with him. Tom recognised that his team would need to talk through periodically how they worked effectively with the new Minister, because some of the causes of the frustration were not going to disappear.

In practice

- What helps you put your frustrations into perspective on a daily and a weekly basis?

- What will help your team put their frustrations into perspective, and how best do you enable that to happen?

- How best do you ensure that time out is used constructively so that you and your colleagues can move on from frustration?

- How best can you use time out to help leave old frustrations behind?

SECTION D
ACT

RECOGNISE WHEN FRUSTRATION CAN LEAD TO POSITIVE CHANGE

FRUSTRATION CAN LEAD TO positive impacts. It is how we respond to frustration that matters.

The idea

William Wilberforce was frustrated by the attitude of business, church and political leaders to the slave trade. He turned that frustration into action. Wilberforce described himself as being 'diligent in the business of life'. The combination of his faith perspective, his humanitarian values and single-minded determination led to an unwavering campaign that resulted in the abolition of the slave trade after years of determined endeavour. When he was frustrated by indifference and indecision, his resolve became stronger. He was determined to reach the end point that he had set himself.

There are many examples of social reformers in the 18th and 19th century who became very frustrated with the way those in power and authority treated humanity. Their frustration led to radical change in health and education provision.

When you are involved in a project or programme, the sources of frustration become a key focus of energy. When these issues are resolved, the project or programme can move forward. Often, the most creative periods are when key frustrations are being addressed and ways forward identified. Innovation often results from bringing insights from other spheres and trying out different approaches.

When frustration surfaces, it can be useful to view it as a positive stimulus for innovative ideas. These are the moments when new thinking can break out and a markedly different new approach developed. In my first career as a senior official in the UK Government, the most creative ways forward emerged from dealing with the most frustrating of situations, because we were forced to come up with new and radically different ways of tackling 'wicked issues'.

Hazel was a recently appointed chief executive of a charity. She had done her due diligence and was concerned that the funding base of the charity was not as robust as the trustees had led her to believe. Soon after she started in post, the income stream began to dip, with the reserves being eaten away. When she presented the latest income figures to the trustees, she made sure that they saw these figures as a wake-up call.

On the one hand, she was frustrated that she had accepted this post when its financial base was not as strong as the trustees had assured her it was. On the other hand, her frustration with the drop in income, and the trustees' awakened frustration that they had not seen the problem coming, led to radical rethinking by both the CEO and the trustees about the priorities of the charity and the need for further innovative fundraising.

In practice

- Remember stories where frustration has led to having the energy and determination to lead positive change.

- Recall when frustration has led to you resolving to make change happen.

- See frustrating situations as opportunities for innovative thinking.

- Allow frustration in situations to build up to the point where there is an openness to new thinking.

ACCEPT THAT SOME FRUSTRATIONS WON'T GO AWAY AND HAVE TO BE LIVED WITH

SOME FRUSTRATIONS ARE UNAVOIDABLE. You cannot pretend they are not there, but you can learn to live with them.

The idea

You may suffer from physical limitations that have to be lived with. You used to be able to climb a mountain quickly, but now you are 'out of puff' part-way up. You used to be able to do mental arithmetic with alacrity, but are now dependent on a calculator. You used to be able to work non-stop for 10 hours a day, but now need respite breaks to recharge your energy. These are frustrations that have to be lived with and won't change.

You may have inherited a team who bring a mixed set of capabilities. They frustrate you by their inability to look very far ahead. The team members have lots of relevant experience and are committed, but you are frustrated that they are not making as much progress as you would like. You recognise that you have to live with the team you have inherited and need to focus on small changes that can make a valuable incremental difference.

Your immediate boss is in post for the next two to three years. You have no say in whether they continue in post. The individual would not be your choice, but you accept that it is not your decision as to who is the CEO of the organisation. You have learnt to rub along with your boss because of their experience and their governance role, which you accept is an essential part of the checks and balances in any organisation.

You may have aspired to hold a more senior position than you currently occupy. You continue to feel frustrated that your ambition has not been completely fulfilled. You tell yourself that in the current role you are able to make a difference in areas that are important to you and provide the income to sustain your family; but you recognise that there will inevitably be an element of frustration that you have to live with when your career has not progressed as you had hoped.

Hazel had accepted the job as CEO of the charity because she was convinced that the charity would be able to make a significant impact in the health arena. The Chair of the organisation was knowledgeable, but somewhat dated in his perspective. The Chair did not fully appreciate the potential impact of modern information technology and was not inclined to move quickly to invest in technological change. Hazel recognised that she would have to take the Chair with her in a measured and relatively slow way.

A couple of her senior team were relatively close to retirement and were not going to radically change their attitude and approach. Hazel talked with them frankly about what they wanted their legacy to be and used this as a means of encouraging them to focus their energy in a constructive way. But they were unlikely to change their broad approach or pace. Hazel recognised that she needed to let them complete their appointments with pride: at the same time she wanted to press them to set their own stretching expectations for their remaining stint at the charity.

In practice

- Be honest with yourself about the people who cause you frustration, and be realistic in recognising where change is possible.

- Accept that you have to live with the frustrations caused by those in authority while not letting those people damage your self-confidence.

- Recognise that frustration is a better alternative to dejected acquiescence.

RECOGNISE THAT YOU NEED TO BE IN THE RIGHT FRAME OF MIND BEFORE YOU CAN ACT EFFECTIVELY

HANDLING FRUSTRATIONS EFFECTIVELY requires you to be in the right frame of mind and not preoccupied with your emotional reactions.

The Idea

In my book, *100 Handling Rapid Change Ideas*, my starting point is that you cannot handle rapid change well unless you are in the right frame of mind. I suggest that key ingredients in bringing the right frame of mind involve recognising why you are in a particular leadership situation, understanding the expectations of others, being ready to be your own barometer of progress, recognising and accepting the risks and accepting the inevitability of surprises and shocks.

Leading well through frustration also involves bringing objectivity and detachment, enabling you to be focused and measured at the same time. You need to be deliberate in your actions, with a clear sense of the opportunities and risks. Seeking to be clear-headed does not mean predicting every eventuality: you have to be ready for the unexpected and be conscious about how you handle on-going uncertainty. The more you have a frame of reference for your actions and are able to articulate to yourself and others why you are taking a particular course of action, the greater the likelihood of progress in addressing and moving on from frustration.

Getting into the right frame of mind will involve understanding and managing your emotions, avoiding getting over-tired, recognising how you will manage stress and keeping your personal energy recharged, especially in a period when frustration may increase rather than diminish.

Hazel recognised that she could get irritated by the Chair and some of her senior team, who could be ponderous. She knew that in order to have a productive conversation with the Chair, she needed to set her expectations reasonably low about making progress. She reminded herself that she needed to begin such conversations in a frame of mind where she was ready to listen to the Chair, as he always made good points, even though they were often clouded with nostalgia.

Hazel accepted that she needed to be patient and persistent with her senior team and not allow herself to become frustrated by their natural conservatism. She recognised that her team would consider evidence carefully, which reinforced in her the importance of using measured evidence rather than rhetoric when she was seeking to persuade them to be more adventurous.

In practice

- Know what helps you achieve a focused and measured approach.

- Align your expectations with how best you handle particular individuals, so that the chances of success are enhanced and disappointment reduced.

- Be alert to how your frame of mind will respond to risks, surprises and shocks.

- Be mindful about when anxiety or stress can disrupt your frame of mind.

RECOGNISE WHEN YOU HAVE BEEN ABLE TO TAKE FORWARD POSITIVE STEPS

LOGGING WHERE YOU HAVE been able to make progress helps provide a secure foundation for next steps.

The idea

If you do not feel you have been able to make any progress in handling your own frustration or the frustration of others, your sense of energy and resolve will inevitably diminish. If you are able to identify some progress, however small, there will be the seed corn of encouragement that will provide you with the hope that future progress is possible.

It helps to set expectations that are stretching but realistic, and then to take pride in progress made, even if that progress feels small. It can take a long time to change the viewpoint of key individuals, but the repetition of sound evidence can lead to small, if somewhat grudging, acknowledgement of some progress.

When frustration is deep-seated, a first step is to accept the reality of that frustration and not let it infect other areas of your life to the extent that it previously did. If the sound of someone's voice sets off a frustrated reaction in you, it can be a measure of progress when your emotional reaction is less acute and you are more able to hold at bay the sense of resentment or anger that might previously have been obvious towards a particular individual.

After three months in her role, Hazel hit a low point. She was equally frustrated with her Chair and some of her leadership team. She felt that they were going to absorb a lot of her time, which would be better deployed focusing on the strategy of the Charity and building key links with partners. She resolved to keep plugging away, seeking to build forward momentum. She resolved not to be daunted by what felt like an uphill approach.

Gradually Hazel began to feel some progress, but recognised it would be slow-going and that major transformation would probably have to wait until the current Chair had moved on. Hazel set her sights fairly low about what could be achieved but was able, over time, to observe some limited progress. She knew it would not be helpful to be negative about the Chair to any of the other trustees or her senior staff. She recognised that she had to work with the Chair and build on the progress achieved. The Chair had appointed her and was committed to her success, which meant that there were moments when she could give feedback to the Chair about the type of leadership she would welcome from him.

In practice

- Set expectations about progress, but do not make them over-ambitious.

- When progress is made, recognise it and seek to make it irreversible.

- Accept that a sequence of small steps can take you a long way.

- Accept that progress is as much about your attitude in responding to frustration as about action taken.

KNOW WHO ARE YOUR ALLIES AND SUPPORTERS

FRUSTRATION ALWAYS APPEARS MORE acute when you feel alone—hence the importance of allies and supporters.

The idea

When you feel frustrated you can easily feel isolated, misunderstood and alone. That sense of isolation can become more acute as frustration builds up. You may want to hide your frustrations from others and build walls around you. You seek to build these defences to protect yourself, but they also have the consequence of inhibiting the building of open relationships with allies and supporters.

You always need some trusted individuals to share your frustrations with. Their presence and support is crucial to your well-being and sense of equilibrium. Spending time with your allies and supporters is one of the best investments you can make as it helps minimise the risks of excessive self-analysis, delusion and self-destruction.

Your allies and supporters are those who have an interest in your success. They may have appointed you, and, therefore, their credibility is at stake. They may have a mutual interest in the successful outcome of the endeavour in which they also share a part.

In whatever organisation you have a leadership role in, it is worth mapping out those who have a shared interest. Some may be your competitors, others your allies. Even your apparent competitors may well be your supporters because of respect for your qualities. Where you think there may be a shared interest, be explicit in building a joint approach that can reinforce the likelihood of progress. When you are frustrated, there is a risk that you can brush aside tentative offers of support from others. Even if your first reaction is not to want the support of others, it is helpful to reflect on your emotional response to see whether there is a mutual interest in joint work that could help reduce your frustrations.

Hazel had built a good relationship with two trustees. These two individuals gave her constructive insights into how best to work with the Chair. Hazel inherited a team coach who had worked with the senior team for a couple of years. This individual gave her good insights into how the team had evolved and how best she could work with individuals about whom she had initially felt apprehensive.

Even though the Chair was causing Hazel some frustrations, she knew that the Chair was committed to her success. What helped reduce Hazel's frustration was the underlying sense that the Chair wanted the arrangements with the new chief executive to work and was committed to improving the effectiveness and reputation of the charity.

In practice

- Be deliberate in cultivating your allies and supporters by sharing your thinking with them at a formative stage.

- Accept that some of the people who might appear competitors are quite likely to be your supporters, too, because of mutual respect.

- Know whom you can talk through your frustrations with in private and trusted conversations.

- Test out how substantive your frustrations are with people you trust.

OBSERVE

OBSERVE HOW OTHERS HANDLE SIMILAR FRUSTRATIONS TO YOURS

Observing how others handle similar frustrations to yours provides potential approaches to how you might best handle the same frustrations.

The idea

In my first career as a civil servant, I observed how a range of different leaders handled frustrations. One would begin to talk very slowly in a measured way as his method of keeping calm. Another was good at identifying three key considerations and summarising the consequences of different risks; she was a clear, analytical thinker and was brilliant at seeing the knock-on consequences of different decisions. Of the government ministers I worked with, one handled frustration by reading poetry, another was highly critical of whoever was the next civil servant entering his office, and a third would pour a gin and tonic.

As well as observing leaders, it is worth asking them what their approach is to handling frustration. It can then be helpful to observe whether their description of how they respond to frustration is borne out by the evidence. The rhetoric and behaviour may not be entirely consistent.

It can be helpful to share experiences with peers about how they have handled similar frustrations. When I was a board member of a government department, we shared openly our frustrations and how we handled them: this helped build up a strong sense of mutual support and encouragement. We sought to look forward, drawing from what we had learnt from listening to each other's experiences.

Abdul was a recently appointed Professor in a university law faculty. He recognised that this post would involve more administration than he had been used to dealing with. He observed how other professors handled their administrative responsibilities. Some ignored them, which eventually led to chaos and very unhappy teaching staff. Other professors had become overwhelmed by the administration work and lost touch with the thought leadership and research dimensions of their responsibilities. Others had sought to box the amount of time they spent on administration, so that priority tasks were dealt with effectively and in a timely way.

Abdul talked through with his professorial colleagues their different approaches to handling administrative tasks. He decided he would use Monday as his administration day and limit the time he spent on administration to half an hour a day on the other days of the week.

In practice

* What are the negative cycles you see some leaders getting into when they become frustrated?

* Who among your contemporaries might you learn from on how they handle similar frustrations to yours?

* What are three lessons you have learnt from people who handle frustration badly?

RECOGNISE HOW THE WAY YOU HANDLE FRUSTRATION AFFECTS OTHERS

THE WAY YOU HANDLE frustration is infectious.

The idea

Whether we like it or not, the way we handle frustration is contagious. If we become edgy, angry or curt, others are likely to either follow a similar pattern or go into avoidance mode. If we become calm, measured and deliberate, others are likely to exhibit similar attributes. The risk, if we become excessively calm, is that some people might think that we do not fully appreciate the significance of an issue—hence the importance of combining calmness with deliberate exploration of an issue.

When your frustration begins to be obvious to others, the biggest risk is that they stand apart metaphorically and physically. In distancing themselves from you they might not be disclosing to you the information or insights you most need to hear and address. They may not be telling you the truth that you need to hear because they do not want to make your angst worse, or suffer the consequences of adverse comment from you.

As a leader, the tone you set in role-modelling how risks are addressed is key to the effectiveness and adaptability of your organisation. It can be helpful to prompt discussion amongst your team about how you will handle moments of frustration. It can be good to explore the risks of negative and unhelpful reactions and how best you enable each other to respond in a constructive way to shocks and surprises. If this is followed by periodic reviews with team members about how the team has responded to frustration, then a continuous learning cycle can be created.

Abdul was conscious that the support team in the law faculty wanted to do their best to ensure his transition to being a full professor ran smoothly. The team were mindful of his time commitments and were deferential to him. Abdul recognised that he was not as structured as he needed to be in his administrative work. He started off by issuing a whole sequence of random requests, with sometimes unrealistic timescales attached to them.

Abdul's frustration with some of the administrative requirements showed in the curt notes he would send to others, which elicited from his peers equally curt responses and from the support staff either excessively long responses or silence. A trusted peer took Abdul out for coffee and gently pointed out that Abdul's frustration was obvious to everyone and that it was proving counter-productive. Abdul needed to be mindful about how his frustration was having a negative effect on both peers and the support team. This was a wake-up call for Abdul, as he had not fully appreciated the amplifying effect that his frustration had on others.

In practice

- What sort of comments have you received about how you have handled frustration in the past?

- What do you observe about the negative consequences on others flowing from how you have sometimes handled frustration?

- What examples can you recall where you have handled frustration well and your approach has been mirrored by others?

- What sort of feedback mechanisms do you have in place to help you be aware of how your frustration is affecting others?

BE MINDFUL OF THE DIFFERENCE BETWEEN CONSTRUCTIVE FRUSTRATION AND RESENTMENT

CONSTRUCTIVE FRUSTRATION INVOLVES a determination to find a positive way forward. Resentment is a self-destructive boiling over of frustration.

The idea

Frustration can grip us. It can lead to powerful, creative, innovative thinking. It can generate the energy to help resolve seemingly intractable problems. But frustration can so easily boil over into resentment if we become preoccupied with the same issue again and again and cannot break out of a cycle of anger or dejection. When frustration becomes resentment it eats away at our well-being. Like an angry boil it needs to be lanced before recovery can begin. Constructive frustration and resentment can initially look very similar. They start from a deeply held sense of frustration and an emotional reaction that demands attention. But an element of resentment can fuel constructive frustration if it is directed in the right way.

For most of us, there will be some occasions when resentment has turned into constructive frustration, and other occasions when resentment has become stuck with a particular story in our minds about the ill-treatment of ourselves or others.

It is worth observing when the language in our head begins to sound like a broken record, with words of anger or frustration repeated again and again. It is worth noting when we have been able to turn a growing frustration or resentment into a more constructive dialogue about what practical steps might be taken to shift apparently immovable obstacles.

Abdul's first reaction when the Head of Department asked him to develop a new programme was frustration about this new expectation when he was just starting to get to grips with his new responsibilities. Initially there was a touch of resentment about this additional expectation—it felt like an unreasonable request to make of someone starting a new role.

Abdul recognised the danger of feeling resentment. A good friend asked him about the opportunities that might flow from designing a new programme. Over a glass of wine Abdul began to talk in a surprisingly enthusiastic way about how he would construct this programme and what sort of students he would want to attract to it. He surprised himself by the constructive way in which he was talking about this new programme. Initially he was holding both a sense of resentment and of excitement about the opportunity. Prompted through further conversations with this friend, he recognised that he needed to leave any sense of resentment behind and move into applying the frustration in a constructive way. This new programme was going to happen, so he had better make it work well.

In practice

- When has an initial sense of resentment turned into a constructive outcome because of the way you dealt with the frustration?

- When have you observed potential resentment in yourself turning into constructive frustration?

- What do you need to do to catch resentment early so it does not become inflammatory?

- What do you observe about turning resentment into constructive frustration?

WATCH IF YOU PROJECT YOUR FRUSTRATIONS ONTO OTHERS

We sometimes assume that others are experiencing the same frustrations as we are, or we blame others for our frustrations.

The idea

When we feel frustrated, we should first address the source of our frustration. It is reassuring to have a reason for our frustrations—it can be attractive to blame others for the frustration we experience. If we feel overworked, we can blame our boss for working in a way that we regard as irresponsible.

We might project our frustrations onto others by assuming they share our attitude, but their personalities and priorities will be different. There might be parallel frustration. But they may be able to live with a misalignment of priorities more readily than us. They may not be as ambitious as we are and, therefore, less likely to feel frustrated.

In the heat of the moment, we can easily assume frustration is equally shared, hence the importance of checking out whether others are as frustrated as you. It might be that they are as frustrated as you, but they are handling it in a different way; or it might be that they have encountered this situation before and bring a longer-term perspective about how solutions work themselves through.

You may be at the point where you are able to turn frustration into constructive thinking about future opportunities and options. It may be that others need more time or evidence before they can reach that enlightened position. It can be worth checking out with colleagues where they are on the cycle of resentment turning into constructive frustration. They may need a constructive nudge before they can join you with similar levels of commitment.

Abdul thought that the support staff would be as frustrated as he was about some of the administrative processes at the university. He thought they would be equally committed to trying to make the processes more up-to-date and efficient. After a while it became clear that many of his colleagues had got so used to the administrative processes that they weren't resentful or frustrated by them. Abdul recognised that he had to adapt his approach to illustrate to them how the processes could be better going forward, allowing more scope for adopting some experimental approaches.

Abdul assumed that some of his professorial peers would be frustrated about the long-term planning for the Law Department. He was disappointed to find that they wanted to take forward future thinking on a slower timetable. Abdul in his enthusiasm in the new post was at risk of becoming frustrated with his colleagues. He recognised that he would have to produce clear evidence to persuade his colleagues that changes were necessary in the way the department operated in order to be able to recruit the right quality of students.

In practice

- When might you be at risk of dumping your frustrations on others?

- How would you know if your assumption that your colleagues experience the same frustrations as you is true or not?

- How best do you understand if the frustrations of your peers align with your frustrations—or are very different?

- How best do you put together clear evidence so that others feel that what is causing you frustration is worth addressing?

SEE THE PATTERN OF YOUR REACTIONS TO FRUSTRATION AS A HELPFUL INSIGHT

As we observe the pattern of our reactions to frustration, it provides insight into how we might respond to similar situations in the future.

The idea

From childhood we have all built up patterns of behaviours in how we respond to different types of situations or stress. We have been conditioned by circumstances and by our own personalities and values into patterns of behaviour that are familiar. Over time, shocks and circumstances alter those patterns, but there is inevitably an underlying rhythm about how we respond to different types of frustration.

As a school pupil, we will have developed a pattern of responding to requests from teachers who have frustrated us. We will have been balancing acceptance and compliance alongside feelings of frustration. This emotional cycle is likely to be embedded and be repeated when authority figures make requests of us. We will have devised different techniques of handling our frustrations, but there is likely to be an underlying pattern that is difficult to change.

It is worth reviewing what has caused you frustration over the last year and how you have handled frustration in terms of both attitude and actions. It is worth reflecting on any evidence that you have been able to adapt your underlying pattern of reactions to frustration, by giving yourself more time to consider options, or through constructive dialogue with others about tricky situations. It can be useful to reflect on how have you deployed evidence in different ways in order to move on constructively from frustration into practical next steps.

Abdul recognised that he could react in an unhelpful way to authority figures. His father had been overbearing and excessively ambitious for his son to become a successful lawyer. Abdul had suppressed the frustration he had often felt about living with these expectations. He had dealt with this frustration by studying hard and cycling long distances. There was a risk that Abdul viewed his Head of Department in the same way as he had viewed his father—i.e., an authority figure who would place strict and potentially unreasonable requests on him.

Abdul recognised that the response of working hard and continuing to do long-distance cycle rides was a helpful approach, but he did not want to be as deferential to his Head of Department as he had been to his father. He knew that the Head of Department had appointed him because they were able to have good, honest debates about the future of legal education. Abdul needed to overcome the feeling that complete deference to this authority figure was the appropriate response. He knew his Head of Department well enough to have a light-hearted conversation about how he responded to authority figures. This helped set the tone for a constructive forward relationship with his boss.

In practice

- What is the pattern of your response when you are frustrated by an authority figure?

- When you are at your best, how do you respond to frustration?

- What are the risks of an adverse response to frustration, and what do you observe in how to best minimise that type of risk?

- What do you observe about how you have been able to modify your reactions to frustration?

SECTION F
REFRAME

BELIEVE THAT GOOD CAN COME OUT OF ANY SITUATION

HOWEVER DIRE THE SITUATION, believe that good can come out of it.

The idea

When an experiment is unsuccessful, the scientist may describe the outcome as a failure or a success. It is a success because he has discovered that one particular method is not providing a solution that works. In an article entitled, 'Embrace failure: it can be a life's best guide' (*The Times*, 18 August 2018), Matthew Parris describes failure, properly handled, as one of the best teachers in life. He talks of the power of failure to redirect a life. He writes: 'Failure weeds out what does not work to give space, air and light to what does. Apply that within one's life and you will see the redeeming power of failure. If only an individual will recognise and respond to it with sufficient ruthlessness. Life is short, be ready to junk what isn't working.'

After a failure, there is a readiness to reassess situations and look at what might be needed going forward. When you are in the midst of paddling through a dark tunnel, there can be a flicker of light that gradually becomes bigger as you approach the tunnel's exit. When a particular course of action is blocked, you have to think laterally about different ways of reaching your desired destination. Failure and blockages force us into a re-evaluation of what is possible and this is often the best stimulus for creative thinking.

When we hold on to a belief that good can come out of any situation, it provides a resolve to keep focused and work through failure or disappointment in order to extract the learning and build clarity about constructive change going forward.

Amanda was the lead minister of a church in a suburban area. It had a reputation as a thriving church that sought to provide a range of activities for people of different ages and interests. A more charismatic church had been established in a neighbouring town and a number of Amanda's church members decided to transfer their allegiance to this new church. Amanda was inevitably disappointed with these departures and had conversations with a number of those leaving.

The departures were a shock to the leadership of Amanda's church. It led to some constructive conversations about prioritisation within the church and how resources could be best deployed. It resulted in positive conversations about how to make the church relevant to the wider community.

In practice

- Always be ready to look for light at the end of the tunnel when going through a tough period.

- See failure as valuable learning about what not to do.

- Recognise that learning flows even more from failure than from success.

- Be deliberate in moving on from your own failures to see future opportunities so that your failures are not a source of frustration.

BE AS DISPASSIONATE AS POSSIBLE ABOUT ISSUES CAUSING YOU FRUSTRATION

THE MORE YOU DEPERSONALISE frustration, the greater the likelihood that you will be able to treat it in a dispassionate way.

The idea

When you are frustrated with an individual, a good way forward is to reflect on the issue that has become the cause of the frustration. The more you can depersonalise the frustration, the greater the likelihood you can handle it in a dispassionate way. The likelihood of finding a solution becomes stronger if the issue is about a decision to be taken and not a personalised interaction between the deeply held views of two individuals. What matters is a successful resolution to an issue, not whether you or the other person wins.

It may not be easy to shift your emotions to a position where progress is all about resolving an issue. When an individual is causing you frustration, it can be helpful to imagine you and this individual seated next to each other on the same side of the table, both looking in the same direction at the issue that needs to be addressed.

Your mindset might be that you have to win a decision in your favour. If you can think about success as whatever approach best addresses the evidence, or a compromise that suits most people, then you are more likely to make progress.

When you feel caught up in a situation causing you frustration, it can be helpful to imagine how an external person would describe what is happening: what would their perspective be? How might you reframe your thinking about a situation to take account of how others, who are not emotionally invested, would view what is happening? Seeing a situation through the eyes of a third party can be a valuable way of enabling you to reframe an issue so that an all-consuming frustration becomes more manageable.

Amanda was frustrated about the variable quality of the music in the church. Her frame of reference had come from a church she had previously been a part of, which had a choral tradition and a legacy of high-quality musical leadership. There was a heritage in the church of encouraging young people to develop their music skills through contributing to public worship.

When Amanda shared this frustration with a couple of leaders, they encouraged her to observe the way young people were building confidence through contributing to the leadership of the music in the church. This helped Amanda reframe her approach. She continued to seek higher levels of musical competence, but recognised the value of giving people the opportunity to develop their skills. Many of the congregation delighted in seeing the young people contributing in this way and were less concerned than Amanda about musical perfection.

In practice

- How best do you focus on the issue to be resolved and not on the person with whom you disagree?

- When you are at loggerheads with an individual who is causing you frustration, how might you describe what is going on in order to depersonalise the situation?

- How open are you to reframing a situation that you find frustrating but which others see as constructive development?

28 BLOCK OUT INTERFERING NOISES IN YOUR HEAD

Interfering noises can distort our judgement and undermine our confidence.

The idea

When we go through a period of frustration, there are inevitably interfering noises in our head. Some will be voices from the past about what it is appropriate to think or do in particular circumstances. There may be constructive voices from mentors who have helped give us the confidence to overcome obstacles.

The voice of reassurance telling us that we can make a difference in any situation can help us be forward-looking when we feel caught in a negative situation. But the negative voices can prevail. There can be a voice in our head saying this is all too difficult; failure is round the corner; this is never going to work; one disaster will follow another. These phrases can loop in our minds and leave us feeling trapped and exhausted. The voices in our head, even when they are negative, can be forewarning us of impending issues. Perhaps we can even befriend the noises, then thank them for their forewarning, park them and move on?

There may be a voice in your head that says, 'This frustration is all your fault.' The voice may be saying, 'You shouldn't have taken this step. You shouldn't have allowed yourself to get into this situation. Your misjudgement is costing you dear.' Perhaps this can be reframed as: 'This bold step was taken for good reason. I have learnt as much from what has worked less well as from what has worked well. I am a stronger person because of what has happened.

I made my initial judgement for the best of reasons. With hindsight, I might have made a different decision, but I made the best decision I could at the time.'

It is worth thinking about how interfering noises can be kept at bay. It might be done through brisk physical exercise or talking with trusted friends. It might be through engaging in activities with the children in your life.

Amanda had a persistent voice in her head that said she could not be as effective as her predecessor. This fear of comparison inhibited Amanda from taking approaches that she thought would work well in the church. She knew that she had to address this interfering noise while at the same time continue to fully respect and acknowledge the leadership contribution that her predecessor had made.

Amanda decided to talk to her predecessor about her ideas for the future. Her predecessor was tactful enough to be enthusiastic about these ideas. The effect was to begin to release Amanda from the interfering noise about comparisons with her predecessor. Not everyone was immediately supportive of her ideas about next steps, but that was fine. She recognised that unanimity was unlikely to be achievable, but she felt she had the blessing of her predecessor and the backing of key people in the church community.

In practice

- Be explicit in naming the interfering noises in your head.

- Be willing to listen to them and then park them.

- Recognise that there will be nuggets of truth that come from the noises.

- Be deliberate in talking through with trusted others whether the noises in your head are illusory or have a grain of truth in them.

BELIEVE THAT A STEP FORWARD IS A STEP FORWARD, HOWEVER SMALL IT IS

PROGRESS COMES A STEP at a time. You are less likely to fall over taking small steps than long strides.

The idea

At the age of 67, Frances and I walked the Machu Picchu trail with our younger son and daughter-in-law. Colin and Holly sped up the steep slopes, apparently undeterred by the high altitude of 4,000 metres. Frances and I walked steadily up the slopes. Frances walked slowly at a regular pace. I walked up 40 steps in one stretch and then gave myself a break. We held on to the belief that if we walked the Machu Picchu trail step-by-step we would reach our destination, which we did.

I was recently told when enquiring about a trail in Nova Scotia that it was difficult and not suitable for seniors. That increased our resolve to do this walk. We set off cautiously but deliberately and reached our destination with time to spare. There are times when a journey seems never-ending or appears difficult. You can learn to reframe that expression of difficulty into one of 'do-ability' if the journey is approached with good planning, at the right pace and with a focus on the outcome.

When climbing a peak, you tackle the immediate hill, and on reaching its brow, you see the next hill that needs to be climbed on the way to the end goal. Experience has taught you that this is the way to get to your destination. You have learnt to reframe your thinking about the first hill as a key marker of progress, even though it is still a long way to the ultimate destination.

A frustration may seem overwhelming and unlikely to be resolved, but if you can reframe it as a frustration that can be addressed in steps, then you are more likely to make some progress. Your frustration about an unresolved issue may seem overwhelming, but if you can reframe it as an issue with a series of components, and you begin to see how you can tackle the first couple of elements, it will then become less daunting.

Amanda wanted to encourage a more ambitious education programme with teenagers. It seemed a daunting task, but Amanda recognised that a key first step was to add to the leadership team a couple of people who were younger than the current leadership. She floated this idea past three or four church members in their late 20s. She did not want to press them too hard, as those taking on this role needed to be passionate about the opportunity it provided. After a number of conversations, one person and then a second agreed to become part of the leadership team.

The next step was to encourage training for the team. Amanda wanted to see results quickly, but had reframed her approach to see one step at a time as progress. It would take two or three years before the young people's group would reach its previous level. She needed determination and patience alongside her belief that there was a clear need to develop this work.

In practice

- Be willing to see small steps as significant progress.

- Do not be browbeaten by people who want to see instant, massive progress when you judge that that is unrealistic.

- Allow yourself to see a long timescale as an accurate description of what success looks like, rather than being second best.

SEE CONTINUOUS LEARNING AS NEVER-ENDING

As some frustrations diminish, others will grow. Our learning about how we handle frustration is never-ending.

The idea

Frustrations change over time. As we get older, there are likely to be frustrations about our physical well-being, but potentially less frustration about unmet ambition. We will have learnt how to address some frustrations—or at least hold them at bay—while other frustrations might grow in prominence.

For a period, you might have been the 'bright young thing' with an impressive future ahead of you. Then other younger people seemed to be passing you by and taking on positions of responsibility that you had previously aspired to. You have learnt how to cope with frustrations resulting from balancing work and responsibilities for a young family. Now you might be balancing commitments to aged parents or grandchildren with work and community activities.

As soon as we stop learning, our frustrations can grow rather than diminish. If our mindset is one of continuous learning, then we are more likely to be ready to tackle new frustrations. If we feel that our learning is done, we can become bogged down by frustrations which, in an earlier phase, we could have handled with reasonable effectiveness.

As we grow older, hopefully our wisdom becomes more astute and we are able to be philosophic about different frustrations and not be overwhelmed by them. We have seen situations before that have caused us frustration and know what works or does not work for us.

We may be called upon to mentor those who are handling frustrations we have experience of. Mentoring younger people and enabling them to learn through different experiences is an excellent way of maintaining continuous learning. As we work with people addressing issues we are familiar with, we are able to remind ourselves of what works for us in handling frustration constructively.

Amanda knew that she had to keep learning in her new role. She could not rely on the approaches she had used in previous churches. Every context was different.

There were new frustrations. She could apply similar approaches to those that had worked for her in the past, but she had to be adaptable and open to continuous learning.

Amanda was dealing with some situations for the first time and refining her approach to situations she had encountered before. Having overall leadership, she could not pass on accountability to others. She and the two church wardens were jointly accountable. They had to recognise that in order to carry their significant accountability well, they needed to be open to addressing new situations and frustrations, in the belief that they had a sense of vocation and a duty to bring an attitude of continuous learning and improvement. Their role was to equip others to take on particular responsibilities whilst holding the overall accountability to the Bishop.

In practice

- What have you learned over the last year about handling frustration, and how are you going to apply that learning going forward?

- How much time are you prepared to invest in continuous learning so that you are keeping abreast of the frustrations that the people you are learning with are experiencing?

- Can you mentor others to help reframe frustration into continuous learning?

31 DISAPPOINTMENT

The idea

A sense of disappointment can stem from childhood, when you might have felt that you were a disappointment to your parents. Your parents may have had high expectations for you, which placed a burden on you. When you had a low mark in an exam or were not successful at sport, you felt you were disappointing your parents. They may have built up the importance of particular events where even though they were showing love and support, you felt that deep down you had caused disappointment to them. Perhaps your parents had been successful in their chosen spheres, and you feared you could not match their achievements. An inner sense of disappointment can be deep-seated and be difficult to cast off.

You want to lead well. You might feel a sense of calling to the work you are doing. At the very least, you want to continue in employment so that there are funds available to look after your family. You want to balance a sense of drive and ambition to do well with an acceptance if life's events do not go your way. Your work may cease or significant personal relationships might come to an end without it being your fault. You are subject to the vagaries of economic, political and commercial change, as well as the personal decisions of those around you.

Handling disappointment is about holding on to what is most important to you and sometimes having to live with disappointment, while seeking to ensure that there are areas in life where you feel you are making progress and can point to successes which have made a difference to the lives of other people.

Jenny taught part-time in a local primary school. Her mother had been a Head Teacher and her father a high-ranking local government official. She had been brought up in a household where her parents were successful. Jenny had received good-quality education with lots of extracurricular activities funded by her parents. Jenny had no desire to be a Head Teacher. She loved working with children in the primary school but did not want promotion. In her early years in teaching, she felt that she had been a disappointment to her parents because she was not ambitious to move up into a management role.

Jenny wrestled with a sense of disappointment that she was not fulfilling the expectations of her parents. She whittled down this sense of disappointment over time and decided to be content with being a classroom teacher for the rest of her teaching career. Just occasionally a sense of inner disappointment raised its head, but she was now mature enough to understand why this happened, reminding herself of the pleasure she gained from having direct contact with her pupils.

In practice

- Seek to understand how deep-seated a sense of disappointment might be.

- Recognise how you have moved on from being gripped by a sense of disappointment.

- Use your story to help others think through the consequences of disappointment in their lives.

32 RELUCTANCE

A RELUCTANCE TO TAKE the plunge or come out of the shadows can lead to individuals not fulfilling their potential.

The idea

Those who are reluctant or hesitant to take on leadership roles will often make the best leaders, as they bring more self-awareness and a good dose of humility. The reluctant leader is more likely to have thought through the consequences of their actions and to be ready for a range of opportunities and skills.

On the other hand, fears and assumptions can prevent us achieving our leadership potential. There can be a hesitancy to step into the unknown. Reluctance can hold us back and then lead to frustration that we have not taken the opportunities available to us. We hold back from contributing in a meeting and become frustrated when others make the points that we wanted to make.

Overcoming frustration caused by reluctance involves recognising your own sources of authority. It involves accepting your right to be at the table and not being overshadowed by your predecessors or others with more experience than you. In our book, *The Reluctant Leader*, Hilary Douglas and I address how to come out of the shadows through believing you can prioritise, learning to engage with 'difficult' people, and being willing to be bold and make decisions. We outline key steps to overcome reluctance, which include giving your rational brain time to catch up with your emotional responses, and bringing clarity to your feelings of reluctance by writing them down or talking them through with trusted others.

The key consideration is: how do you use the frustration you feel to help you be more bold next time? Perhaps it involves taking risks by putting a proposition on the table or contributing earlier in a meeting.

Harriet got increasingly frustrated that in meetings she was reluctant to contribute and did not have the impact that she or her boss wanted her to have. She kept holding back when others were contributing. Harriet had loads of ideas but did not want to embarrass herself by speaking up. The more frustrated she became about not contributing, the less comfortable she felt intervening. She was on a downward spiral in terms of confidence.

What made a difference was a couple of meetings where the Chair drew her in early. The Chair made clear that she wanted to hear Harriet's views. After she had made her contribution, the Chair built on those comments in taking forward the meetings. Harriet began to feel liberated to contribute in a way that she had not done before. At last she felt that she could speak her mind. Looking back, she recognised the role the Chair had taken in encouraging her to break through the barrier of reluctance, which had previously seemed impermeable.

In practice

- Be willing to take a risk and say what you think.

- Recognise your sources of authority and believe that people want to hear what you want to say.

- Accept your right to be at the table and do not be overshadowed by those with apparently greater experience than you.

- Believe that the frustration caused by reluctance can be addressed successfully, as many people before you have shown.

RESENTMENT

RESENTMENT CAN EAT AWAY at our sense of well-being and may be difficult to tackle because we hide it.

The idea

Reluctance is an internal frustration that we may choose to be open about and discuss with colleagues. Resentment, on the other hand, is something we might feel guilty about. We can feel that it is somehow wrong to be resentful and, therefore, we seek to suppress the emotion and don't want to admit that we are gripped by resentment.

The inner sense of resentment might come from feeling that we have been misjudged or ill-treated. We can feel resentful about a lack of success, finance, achievement or good relationships. Resentment can burn inside us and eat away at our sense of creativity because it blinds us to future possibilities.

Resentment is a difficult subject to talk about. We are only likely to be open about it with those we particularly trust. When the feeling is deep-seated, conversations with a counsellor can unlock some of the reasons for the resentment and allow us to begin to move on. It can take some years for a sense of resentment to erode to a point where it becomes incidental and then irrelevant. Resentment about mistreatment will often leave a scar that will never be completely removed and has to be lived with.

John felt he had been promised promotion as a reward for doing a demanding role, but promotion never came. He resented the false promises he had been given. All the hard work he had put into this demanding project had come to nothing. It had exhausted him, leaving him at risk of feeling resentful. He gradually and grudgingly accepted the lack of early promotion, but when it did not happen three years later the sense of resentment doubled. He felt that the bosses had acted with duplicity. He felt he had been used by the organisation and was not appreciated.

Over time, John became more and more resentful, with his demeanour looking downcast. The resentment was showing and he didn't care. The consequence was that John was regarded as someone who was out of date and had not moved with the times. His resentment was just below the surface and colleagues felt it might burst out at any moment. John sought to keep the resentment under control, but the resentment fuelled frustration that drained his energy and meant his performance was not as sharp as it used to be. He was now a long way from being promoted.

In practice

- Admit to yourself what you feel resentful about.

- Be willing to talk frankly to one or two trusted people about the frustration caused by resentment; but be very selective about who you discuss this with.

- When a particular situation fuels your resentment, be ready to move to work in a different context where you can have a fresh start.

34 PESSIMISM

PESSIMISM CAN STOP US doing foolish things, but can also create unnecessary frustration that saps our energy.

The idea

Every team benefits from having one pessimist who can be guaranteed to see the problems and darker side of every situation. A resident pessimist can help put optimism and passion into context, but pessimism, when it takes a grip, can be insidious, sapping hope and aspiration.

Pessimism can flow from a natural cautiousness or previous bad experiences. When a particular approach to solving a problem has been tried on a number of occasions and not worked, pessimism can grow. The pessimist in you wants to give up hope and is not open to the possibility of breakthroughs and a new awakening.

When pessimism creeps into your thinking, it can be worth asking yourself what insights it brings to the situation. What are the three key messages that the pessimist wants to tell me? It can be helpful to allow yourself to be the pessimist for 30 minutes and explore every eventuality from a pessimistic viewpoint. That can be followed by 30 minutes when you view the same situation from an optimistic perspective. You are likely to end up with two very different scenarios, which will give you the opportunity to compare different outcomes.

A corrective to pessimism is to recall on how many occasions your pessimism has been misplaced. Thinking about the worst thing that can happen in a meeting or a conversation can prepare you for the worst outcome—and remind you that the worst outcomes are not life-threatening. We can overdo the negative consequences that might result from pessimism and believe they are inevitable; on the other hand, pessimism grounds us in the harsh reality of some eventualities.

Barbara grew up in a family where her parents were pessimistic about everything, from the government to the weather. Conversations at the dinner table were about what might go wrong next. Barbara was brought up to think that pessimism was a natural way of thinking. Barbara accepted that the world was never as dark as her parents suggested and had grown into a bright and cheerful adult. But she knew how to switch on the pessimism button and used this skill to good effect when the team was examining risks and considering the downsides of different approaches.

Barbara was careful not to be gripped by the dark side of pessimism. She could appear to others to be a pessimist because she could express the pessimist view clearly, but she became frustrated with pessimists because she felt they were caught in a spiral of negativity that could be destructive. The paradox was that Barbara could express the pessimist view perfectly but was more frustrated by pessimism than any of her colleagues. This flowed from her experience of pessimism as a child.

In practice

- Allow the pessimist in you to help identify the potential risks and adverse consequences of a project.

- Sit the pessimist alongside the optimist to get a more balanced perspective.

- Be aware of the risk of pessimism causing frustration in others if it is given too much credibility.

35 OVER-OPTIMISM

A SENSE OF OPTIMISM keeps us fresh and forward-looking, but too much optimism can mean reality is ignored.

The idea

Cultivating a positive mindset involves believing that no matter how intractable a challenge might be, there is a way out of it. It is about focusing on what can be done going forward, not what has gone wrong. Leaders who have navigated effectively through turbulent times emphasise the importance of having grounded optimism rather than false optimism. Grounded optimism requires a constructive mindset combined with healthy realism about what is going on around you. Grounded optimism draws on past experience, current evidence and the belief that constructive forward steps can be identified. Grounded optimism involves the belief that a difficult situation can be transformed.

False optimism is the product of asserting something without underlying evidence. There are moments when a leader needs to be optimistic without strong evidence, but to be convincing there needs to be some underlying rationale that people can grasp.

Excessive optimism may generate energy in the short term but often leads to frustration in the long term. Someone who is perpetually over-optimistic is unlikely to have dedicated followers. The frustration that results from over-optimism flows from a combination of disappointment in one's own judgement and a lack of long-term commitment and support from others.

Over-optimism is best avoided through balancing a belief in positive change with healthy realism. It involves examining both the evidence that progress is possible as well as the potential risks. The frustration flowing from the disappointment of over-optimism can be addressed through being as dispassionate as possible in assessing facts and evidence, whilst maintaining the belief that constructive change is attainable.

Rob was a firm believer that good could come out of any situation. The risk was that he bolstered his view by brushing aside evidence that was inconsistent with his preferred approach. He could come over as cavalier in dismissing cautious views. His relentless optimism was inspiring to some, but others were wary of his judgement.

Colleagues tended to keep their distance and keep their own counsel rather than trust Rob's judgement. Rob felt undermined by this suspicion towards him. He became increasingly frustrated with this distrust. His initial response was to become even more optimistic, which made the situation worse and created further frustration. Slowly, he came to recognise that he needed to be much more evidence-based in advocating ways forward.

In practice

- What does grounded optimism mean for you?

- How best do you root optimistic views in shared experience and evidence?

- How best do you handle your frustration when you believe you are advocating grounded optimism and others are sceptical?

- How best do you handle a sense of disbelief and distrust from others when you are putting forward an optimistic perspective?

36 | ANIXETY

ANXIETY

TIREDNESS THAT FLOWS FROM anxiety can lead to exasperation.

The idea

For a period of two or three years I woke regularly at 4 a.m., worried about the decisions I needed to make or the consequences of decisions I had taken. I kept going over in my mind potential adverse consequences of wrong decisions. I was at risk of being in the grip of anxiety. As I travelled on the 7.24 a.m. train to London, I had a more rational view of the issues and was able to plan next steps in a way that was not possible at 4 a.m.

This sense of anxiety was reducing how much time I slept. The persistent waking up early felt like a damaging blow to my well-being. I was not sure what was more damaging: the anxiety, or my frustration about my anxiety. Holidays and weekends helped, as the early morning waking was limited to working days, but the relentless shorter nights took a toll on my freshness of thinking.

Many other people have had a similar experience. We do not want to admit this biting sense of anxiety, but it is there nonetheless. It cannot be overcome easily. A change of role might be needed to eradicate the anxiety. Defining responsibilities and expectations more clearly can help. Recognising the particular stimulus that sets off anxiety can forewarn us of impending issues.

The frustration that flows from anxiety can be difficult to manage, especially if the sources of anxiety are not going to go away. Anxiety about personal relationships and the health of people close to you cannot be ignored. Anxiety about the children in your life evolves as the children grow into adults.

Anxiety about work may not be possible to change. Being explicit about the causes of anxiety and talking them through with trusted others can help put them in perspective—but progress is inevitably going to be limited, with the frustration needing to be managed rather than eradicated.

Helen felt perpetually under pressure in her work. Expectations were put on her by a variety of different people. She tried to handle the 4 a.m. syndrome by keeping a notebook next to her bed in which she wrote down briefly the practical steps she was going to take the following day to address an anxiety that was bothering her. Helen deliberately tried to go to bed by 10.15 p.m. to ensure she got a decent amount of sleep. She recognised that getting up at 6 a.m. was better for her than tossing and turning until 7 a.m. She was able to talk through her anxiety with a trusted friend. This helped, but did not eradicate the frustration caused by the anxiety.

In practice

- Be honest in identifying the causes of your anxiety.

- Recognise at what time of day you are best able to think about positive steps to handle a particular anxiety.

- Accept that anxiety will cause a level of frustration, and work out ways to manage that frustration.

- Try to distinguish between anxieties you can do something about and those that remain beyond your control.

37 PHYSICAL PAIN OR DISABILITY

THERE IS ALWAYS LEARNING from how those suffering physical pain or handling disability cope with frustration.

The idea

Two of the people I have worked closely with have been wheelchair-bound. They manage their journeys to work and their contribution at work superbly. They do not let their physical disability get in the way of either. They rightly expect chairs to be moved so they can sit at the table with their colleagues. They do not expect preferential treatment in the way their views are considered. They have learned to handle the frustration of having a physical disability.

Two other people I work with are deaf and rely on lip-reading. They receive supportive comments regularly from their colleagues who want to involve them fully in meetings, but the discipline of always looking at them when you are contributing in a meeting is less easy to sustain. These two individuals are continually having to live with the frustration that they cannot hear everything clearly. One of them rightly keeps reminding people to look at her when they speak. The other is too polite to do so, which means that meetings are a frustrating experience for her.

A lot of physical pain is invisible and, therefore, colleagues are not continually reminded that they need to make allowance for the pain someone might be enduring. The individual suffering from acute back pain does not want to keep grimacing, or moving around to relieve the discomfort, because they do not want to draw attention to themselves or disrupt the flow of a meeting.

Physical pain inevitably causes frustration, but it is legitimate to be open about what needs to happen to help to reduce that frustration. It is important not to be shy about sharing how the frustration of physical disability or pain is best managed so that an individual can contribute fully to discussions.

Henry had recently broken his leg in a skiing accident and was walking using crutches. He returned to work as soon as he could because he did not want to let his colleagues down. Moving around was slow and could be painful. He thought he might be frustrating his colleagues by his slowness and the way he had to sit in meetings. He soon realised he was far more frustrated than his colleagues were—they were delighted to have him back at work. Because of the acceptance by the people he worked with, Henry's own frustration rapidly diminished. He accepted that the limitation on physical movement was something that he was going to have to live with for the next few weeks.

In practice

- What do you admire most about those who handle physical disability or pain at work?

- How have you best handled the frustration of physical pain in the past?

- How best do you create an environment whereby those who have physical disability or pain are not frustrated by custom and practice?

38 ANGER

Righteous indignation can be a frustration that leads to constructive outcomes, while relentless anger is inevitably destructive.

The idea

Anger is one of the most destructive forces affecting any team. Trust takes a long time to build up. Anger can destroy trust in an instant. I have observed situations where anger between one individual and another, with emotive words being used to describe an individual's approach, has been hugely destructive and not easily forgotten. Once someone has been described as 'greedy', the word is unlikely to be forgotten. Inevitably when someone has been described with emotive words which question their integrity they are likely to be wary of the individual who has offended them and limit the degree of trust they are willing to place in them. Only an abject apology for the excessive use of emotional language can redeem such a situation.

Anger flows out of frustration but can create far greater frustration than the cause of the initial issue. Anger about a person is almost inevitably destructive. Anger about a situation can lead to constructive change. Righteous indignation can be a force for good in focusing on necessary changes, but it is far more likely to be effective if the indignation is directed at the issue rather than an individual. You might be angry about how particular people are being dealt with. Verbal attacks on the individual who is leading that group might be your preferred approach, but success may be more likely if the righteous indignation is focused on changes that are needed that will benefit the whole organisation and not just the people who you think are being mistreated.

When we are in the grip of frustration caused by our own anger, we need to watch the damaging effect that the expression of that frustration can have on those closest to us. Having a well-rehearsed method of turning anger into physical exercise can be an effective way of keeping that anger at bay and reducing its destructive consequences.

Bob knew that anger could boil up in himself when he thought the Finance Department was acting irresponsibly. When they said no to his reasonable requests, he wanted to tell them directly that they were incompetent. He knew that he had to hold back this angry, frustrated reaction. He needed to stand back and reflect on the evidence. Was this an issue on which there was clear justification for the expenditure, or did he need to accept the judgement of his finance colleagues because of other pressures on them? Bob knew he had to deploy his rational self to dilute the anger he experienced every time he received an e-mail from the Finance Department.

In practice

- See righteous indignation as a source of energy and resolve.

- Observe in yourself the potential for anger before it bursts out and causes collateral damage.

- When you are angry, focus your comments on the issue and not the individual who is causing you frustration.

- Remember the damaging consequences that can flow if you lose control.

- Be ready to apologise if anger gets the better of you.

39 | FEELING STUCK

When you feel stuck, you are frozen in your own frustration and need to thaw out.

The idea

Feeling stuck is one of the most debilitating of frustrations. You see no exit from your current situation. You may feel that you are in a loveless marriage, in a declining organisation or a thankless enterprise. Many coal miners used to feel stuck in their jobs. There were limited other sources of employment in the locality and these did not pay as much as being a coal miner.

The miners felt stuck in a form of work with inherent danger and inevitable damage to their long-term health. The arduous, physical nature of their work exhausted them. Their frustration could express itself in militant union activity. But frustration could also be expressed in joyful engagement in music, through male voice choirs or brass bands. Frustration in their work could have the knock-on effect of creative, exuberant involvement in music and sport.

When you feel stuck, it can be like being in a locked room with no windows. There is no light and shade. The scope for movement seems non-existent. You long for things that will unblock this sense of stuckness without much hope that they will happen. You seek to find alternative sources of respite and joy, accepting that certain core areas of your life are going to feel stuck for the foreseeable future. Stuckness is just the way it is, and you learn to live with that frustration and focus on other outlets that give you a feeling of worth and joy.

Georgina felt stuck in a difficult marriage and a boring job. Her husband seemed dependant on alcohol, which caused him to become either aggressive or morose. For the sake of the children, Georgina decided to stick with the marriage for the moment. She was competent at the work she did at a local government office, but saw little prospect of promotion. She did not push herself to do an outstanding job and, therefore, was not considered when promotion opportunities arose. This double frustration was something Georgina felt she had to live with. The biggest joys for her were seeing her children grow and being part of a local choir. She felt uplifted and inspired when singing with fellow members of the choir.

Georgina felt locked in. She hoped one day that her husband would be open to having counselling about his alcohol dependency and was ready to choose the right moment to suggest this. When a sympathetic boss encouraged her to think about the possibility of taking on another area of responsibility that would give her a higher profile, she reluctantly agreed. She began to admit to herself that she need not feel quite as boxed in at work. Maybe there were ways of handling the frustration of being stuck that could be taken forward.

In practice

- In what areas of your life do you feel stuck?

- Is that stuckness inevitable, or can you see a way of shifting the stuckness?

- In what areas of your life are you free and unstuck, and how can you develop those areas further?

- What might happen over the next few months to reduce that sense of stuckness and can you fast-forward these potential enablers?

40 FEELING MISUNDERSTOOD

WE CAN FEEL TYPECAST by our previous views or actions, with this legacy holding us back.

The idea

The individual who is associated with a particular failure may become typecast. The view that other people have of them is frozen in time by virtue of one outstanding result or a debacle that people are reluctant to forget. The scientist who took forward a particular innovation in their early 30s may be continuing to offer new ideas in their 50s, but other people want to keep talking about the innovation from 20 years earlier. The scientist gets frustrated that no one seems to be interested in his new ideas and just want him to go over ground he has discussed hundreds of times before.

You may be very good at seeing the risks in a particular situation. The consequence might be that your colleagues see you as negative and wanting to slow progress down. You might feel misunderstood when your intention is that you want to help the organisation move forward constructively in the light of—and not in ignorance of—risks and constraints. Sometimes you feel you have to keep repeating your positive commitment to the endeavour, so that you do not get misrepresented as a negative critic.

Sometimes you might feel that others deliberately distort what you have been doing, to either bolster their case or undermine yours. This could flow from deliberate distortion, or it could result from others looking through such a different lens from your own that they do not see the relevance of your perspective.

When you feel misunderstood, patience and persistence are called for. Patience will help you choose the right moment to address how others have misunderstood you. Persistence will allow you to be firm in putting across your view so that it is properly understood.

Rashid brought a lot of experience of what works in terms of social change in communities. He was part of a local government taskforce with colleagues who brought bright ideas about direct intervention. Rashid kept talking about how best to win the hearts and minds of people in local communities. His colleagues felt that his approach would take too long. They wanted more direct intervention and investment, bringing in projects that had worked elsewhere.

Rashid patiently built up a relationship of trust with his colleagues and introduced them to people in the community. He was persistent in advocating a much more consultative approach. He had felt misunderstood by his colleagues initially, but through his persistence they recognised his wisdom. Rashid had not let his initial frustration get in the way of shifting the thinking of this project group into a more constructive space.

In practice

- When you feel misunderstood, think about why that might be happening.

- Appreciate the perspective that others bring and how that might explain why you feel misunderstood.

- Be patient and persistent in advocating what you think is the right course of action.

- See the frustration of feeling misunderstood as something you can change over time.

LIVING WITH PAST MISJUDGEMENTS

PAST MISJUDGEMENTS CAN BE our greatest source of insight; they need not be the cause of continuous frustration.

The idea

If we have not made misjudgements, we have not lived. If we feel paralysed about making decisions, we are in effect choosing to not make a decision. We make judgements all the time and inevitably some will be wrong.

We observe some people who have moved on from misjudgements and have created a new life that has worked effectively. The misjudgement might have been about a business enterprise that became bankrupt or a career choice that proved to be a wrong step. We can feel caught by these misjudgements for a period. The question is: can we move on and learn from misjudgement, and begin a new approach that is not tainted by past, negative experiences? Can previous misjudgements be a source of strength in ensuring that our sense of discernment becomes more acute, so that we are not in the grip of damaged self-esteem flowing from past misjudgements?

Frustration about past misjudgements will recur from time to time. Financial investments that proved to be folly were done for the best of reasons. Remembering why you made decisions at the time can help you diminish frustration that flows from past judgements.

Some misjudgements we are stuck with—it may be too late to change your career and unrealistic to move to a different location. Moving on from other misjudgements is a matter of choice, where courage is needed to make difficult decisions that cause short-term pain but which potentially bring long-term freedom and new hope.

James had gone into banking as a career because he had strong numeracy skills and it paid well. But as the number of people employed in local banking declined, he knew he had to think about other alternatives. He was cross with himself about the misjudgement of going into banking, but he had not appreciated at that time the effect that internet banking would have on local banking staffing levels and opportunities.

A friend pressed James to think through what in his heart of hearts he would love to do. The friend asked James to score instinctively out of 10 how attracted he was to different areas of work. Local government scored three, social services scored two, charity work scored four. Then James surprised himself by scoring teaching as nine. This instant assessment gave James a clue about potentially exploring the possibility of moving from banking to teaching.

James remembered a couple of former colleagues who had moved into teaching. He spoke with them about what they had experienced in their career transition and decided to take a redundancy package from the bank and enrol in a teacher-training programme. The experience in banking had given him an understanding about the numeracy requirements of the next generation and the dynamics of operating in a small, local organisation.

In practice

- See misjudgements as an inevitable part of life.

- Recognise the learning that flows from misjudgements and how that informs your future.

- Allow your frustration about past misjudgements to help you think through future options.

- Consider how best you can break out of the grip of past misjudgements.

42 FEELING UNDERVALUED

FEELING UNDERVALUED CAN ERODE our self-confidence and self-worth to the point where we need to give ourselves a good talking-to.

The idea

Feeling undervalued is part of life. Parents of teenagers feel undervalued by their children. The unseen workers who provide electricity and water for our homes can feel undervalued by demanding customers. Hardworking members of a charity feel undervalued by the trustees or the recipients of the work at the charity. We have all developed ways of coping with the sense of feeling undervalued. We put up with it when the children in our lives undervalue us. We shrug our shoulders and are accepting when our busy boss does not recognise our contribution.

There are occasions when it is helpful that nobody is drawing attention to what we are doing. We want to be a hidden presence that is seeking to enable an organisation to function well. We want to be good neighbours to those people in our community who are suffering or who need practical help. We know in our own minds the value we are contributing and don't need reassurance or affirmation from others.

On other occasions we feel that some acknowledgement of our contribution is appropriate. We want to believe that others think we are making a difference. Perhaps sometimes we can be too needy for approval and could rely more on our own judgement about whether a contribution is helpful. When you begin to feel frustrated about feeling undervalued, it is worth considering why you want that affirmation. Can you tell yourself that affirmation from others is not needed because you know you are doing the right thing? With this perspective your level of frustration might be reduced.

Gillian felt at risk of being undervalued by her family and her colleagues. She accepted that her teenage children were not going to recognise her contribution. But she could not allow any frustration with her teenage children to get in the way of her fully supporting them in all they did. When Gillian did not feel fully valued at work, she chose moments to be explicit about the contributions that she and her team had made. She unashamedly drew attention to progress that had resulted directly from the commitment of her team.

Gillian was deliberate in deciding that her frustration with her teenage children needed to be contained within her own heart, whereas she needed to express her frustration about the team's contribution not being fully valued within her organisation. Gillian was not going to let herself down by showing frustration with her teenage children, and she was not going to let her team down by accepting the undervaluing of the team within the organisation.

In practice

* Recognise why you are being undervalued in some situations.

* Be deliberate in choosing when to address that sense of being undervalued and when to let it pass.

* When you are frustrated about being undervalued, turn it into affirmation of the whole team of which you are part.

* Accept that you are the best judge of the value of your contribution.

43 SELF-CRITICISM

SELF-CRITICISM IS VALUABLE WITHIN limits, but potentially destructive when given a free rein.

The idea

Good leaders will regularly review what they could do differently next time. They are continually exploring how they have impacted particular situations and in what way they might use their experience and insight in more constructive ways. A valuable way of focusing on continuous improvement is to ask yourself at the end of a week: what two things did I learn this week and what two things might I do differently next week?

Self-criticism carries the risk that we beat ourselves up. We can be our own worst enemy in castigating ourselves for our errors. Excessive self-criticism can get in the way of learning and developing. If we say to ourselves that we are never going to be able to handle a particular situation well, we create a self-fulfilling prophecy about our apparent incompetence.

Relentless self-criticism is exhausting for ourselves and others. Those who love us may eventually become exhausted, bored or overwhelmed by the self-criticism. Ultimately they may have little choice other than to leave us to wallow in our own self-destructive absorption.

Reducing the frustration resulting from self-criticism requires putting self-criticism in a wider context. It can be helpful to sit in a chair and allow yourself to be self-critical, then move to a different chair, where you describe your qualities and the progress you have made. This physical movement from one chair to another can help you see both the learning that can come out of the self-criticism and the wider application of your qualities.

Juliette was at risk of beating herself up at the accountancy practice where she was a senior partner because it was not as financially strong as it used to be. She was very self-critical about some of the decisions she had made about people, strategy and marketing. She forced herself to recognise that the decisions she had taken had increased the quality of the work of the practice and ensured that its back office support was much more efficient.

Juliette accepted that her self-criticism was excessive, but she still felt in the grip of it and found it hard to cast off. She recognised that she needed the affirmation of her colleagues in order to put her self-criticism in context. Thankfully, the other partners recognised the positive actions she had taken and were appreciative in acknowledging the value of her leadership.

In practice

- See self-criticism as an important part of development.

- Be aware of the risk of self-criticism turning into self-flagellation.

- Always set personal criticism alongside affirmation of progress made.

- See some frustration flowing from self-criticism as generating the commitment to change.

- Walk away from self-criticism when it begins to feel unrelenting.

44 LACK OF SELF-BELIEF

The idea

We do not want to appear aggressive or overbearing. We observe others who seem full of their own importance and authority. We do not want to mirror their behaviours. We want to shape our own self-belief and action in a way that is responsible and effective in drawing out the best in others and not squashing them.

We recognise the importance of self-belief in the children in our lives so that they are confident entering different situations and are able to contribute with a diverse group of contemporaries. We observe how some people through lack of self-belief close themselves off and become isolated. Their sense of self-belief rapidly diminishes and their confidence collapses. We notice how someone's self-belief dissipates if they have a long-term illness. Observing people afflicted by a lack of self-belief can be a warning to us to hold on to a proper sense of self-belief and self-worth for the sake of our own well-being and mental health.

We may notice situations where a lack of self-belief can hit us starkly. We recognise that we need to prepare for those situations carefully. With some individuals, we might feel tongue-tied and unable to be at our best. Frustration about being in their presence sets off an inability to express our views coherently. We are at risk of feeling completely overawed by people who want to engage with us and hear our perspective.

Rosemary was fine in front of a classroom of noisy children. She was confident, engaging and effective in this context. The children were learning well through her enthusiastic, thoughtful teaching. But when Rosemary stood in front of a group of adults, her confidence dropped through the floor. She was not self-conscious in a classroom of children as her confidence flowed naturally through what she did; but facing a sea of adults set off deep-seated unease about whether they would take her seriously. This inhibition had held her back from applying for senior posts at schools when all the other indicators were positive about the likelihood of success.

Rosemary knew she had to tackle this hesitancy and deliberately put herself in situations where she would be leading conversations with 10 or 12 adults. She had practised this approach in her church, getting used to being a leader of a home group. Rosemary sought to build up confidence and self-belief so she could come over authentically with a group of parents. She offered to lead a session with parents about reading with their children; this worked well and gave her a new level of confidence.

In practice

- In which situations is your self-belief at its strongest and why?

- Are you able to anticipate when a drop in your self-belief is about to happen?

- Who can you work with to help you address frustration that can flow from a lack of self-belief in some situations?

- What small steps can you take to address your role in situations where your self-belief is at risk?

IMPOSTER SYNDROME

THE IMPOSTER SYNDROME CAN strike like a bolt of lightening which hits in a devastating way.

The idea

Sometimes you can take delight in being in a situation that you had never expected. You feel blessed about your friendships, the community in which you live, the work you do and your colleagues. On other occasions you feel like a complete imposter with no credibility. You feel that you have been found out. You have no right to be present and have none of the qualities needed to make a success of your current role. You feel gripped by inadequacy.

The imposter syndrome can occur at any moment and cause inner turmoil and frustration. You want to escape and run a mile, or you want to hide away. Nursing yourself back to health after a bout of imposter syndrome takes time and careful handling. You need to be kind to yourself and talk with those who will help nurture you back to your normal self.

The imposter syndrome can have a crippling effect and stop someone from making constructive decisions. After a while their limited effectiveness becomes obvious and their role becomes questionable. This 'proves' to them that feeling like an imposter is justified and that they should never have been holding this level of responsibility in the first place.

The imposter syndrome can produce this self-fulfilling consequence, hence the importance of being deliberate in addressing the effect of such a lightning strike. You cannot just wish it away. It requires recognising why you are in the position you are in, the qualities you bring, why people appointed you, and the progress you have made.

Ben always appeared confident as a police superintendent, but there were moments when he felt a complete fraud. He had to keep telling himself that he had built a successful career in the police force and had been promoted on merit to his superintendent role. He was well thought of by the senior officers and had long-term potential, but this did not stop him feeling a fraud sometimes.

The police officers were deferential towards him, but he wondered what they really thought. He had never aspired to be a police superintendent, as he had been content first as a constable and then as a sergeant. He was not sure whether he wanted the additional responsibilities, but he could see where he had deployed police officers well and had ensured that crime rates had been tackled effectively. A lot of positive things had happened under his watch. But he recognised that from time to time the imposter syndrome would strike and he would have to hold his nerve until the feeling passed.

In practice

- Accept that in some situations you are at risk of feeling an imposter.

- Seek to prepare how you will respond in such a situation.

- Recognise how best you can hold your nerve when the imposter syndrome strikes.

- Be willing to share your stories about how you have handled situations when the imposter syndrome strikes as a means of helping others handle similar moments of self-doubt.

SECTION H
FRUSTRATIONS CAUSED
BY OTHERS

46 | RESPONSIBILITY WITHOUT AUTHORITY

Holding responsibility may be fine, but with limited authority responsibility can turn into an unrealisable burden.

The idea

Responsibility and the authority to act need to go together. When you are given responsibility, you need to know the discretion you have in using resources and making decisions. You do not want to be burdened with unrealistic expectations or with constraints that inhibit the delivery of those expectations. You recognise that you cannot have a completely free rein as there will be accepted procedures that need to be followed and good practice that needs to be observed.

When asked to take on responsibility, it is crucial to carry out due diligence about the resources at your disposal and the degree of discretion you have so you understand what is achievable and where you might struggle to deliver on expectations. It is always worth pushing back to build clarity about the level of resources available, so that you can reach agreement about what can be delivered under your responsibility.

Sometimes you accept responsibility without knowing the underlying issues. The competition might be more severe than you had anticipated. Unpredictable events might delay progress. Some valued staff might move elsewhere. When you accept responsibility there are bound to be uncertainties, but in dealing with those uncertainties you do not want to be fettered by unreasonable restrictions, so you need to be clear about what you have control over and the limits of your power.

When you find there are unexpected limits on your discretion that affect your ability to deliver, it is worth asking questions about why, and seeking to push the boundaries. Key will be the type of evidence you can bring to justify your being given greater authority needed to enable you to deliver on your responsibilities.

Nathan was asked to lead a project introducing a new IT system. It rapidly became clear that the constraints on recruitment would inhibit delivery on the expected timescale. Nathan set out his predicament to the HR Department, who were concerned about setting precedents that could be used by other parts of the business.

Nathan was clear with both his boss and the HR Director that a significant delay in recruitment would have an effect on the delivery of the new system. He put his case rationally and carefully. He did not allow a sense of frustration with the recruitment procedures to stop him expressing in a dispassionate way the consequences of different approaches. He presented this as a shared problem for the business and was given some concessions on recruitment that made the prospects of delivering on the tight timescale stronger.

In practice

- Be wary of accepting responsibility when you are not clear about your degree of authority.

- Seek a clear understanding with your boss and key departments about your level of discretion.

- Provide choices about what can be delivered depending on different levels of resources, rather than threatening a complete debacle if your wishes are not met.

- Be aware of using your frustration about having responsibility with limited authority as an excuse for not taking the necessary action.

REJECTION

WHEN PEOPLE STOP listening to you, shouting doesn't help.

The idea

We all have survival mechanisms that sometimes include rejecting or blanking out people who cause us pain or who ask us difficult questions. We pretend they don't exist as a means of protecting ourselves. We may take this blinkered approach in order to survive in difficult situations. We should not, therefore, be surprised when other people use the same approach in relation to us. If we represent a different point of view or are putting forward counter-arguments to theirs, their response may be to reject us and our views and not engage with us.

Parents of teenagers know that there may well be periods when teenagers reject their advice. These painful periods have to be lived through; they normally come to an end after a season, perhaps an extended season.

The feeling of rejection by your colleagues is painful and damaging to your self-worth. Sometimes you have to respond quickly to assert your authority. The representative from the Finance Department will not find it acceptable that their views are rejected and will insist on their perspective being taken into account.

On other occasions it may be right to let that sense of rejection continue for a short period. It might be that the person who you think is rejecting you is focused on urgent tasks, which means that they may be appearing to ignore you—hence the importance of choosing the right moment to approach them, and discover whether it is a more systematic, longer-term rejection.

Barbara felt rejected by her boss because he kept cancelling their catch-up conversations. The frustration caused by feeling rejected had been building up in her. A peer gently pointed out to her that the crisis that her boss was dealing with elsewhere was inevitably taking a lot of time and energy. It was not surprising that her boss was not available to talk with her on a regular basis. The fact that her boss kept cancelling the one-to-ones was a mark of respect to Barbara. He was trusting Barbara to deal with her area of responsibility.

What Barbara had interpreted as rejection was more an affirmation that she was doing the right thing. She needed to turn that sense of frustration about apparent rejection into a belief that she was trusted to get on with her job.

In practice

- When you feel rejected, reflect on whether you are actually being rejected or whether other priorities have taken precedence.

- See apparent rejection as potentially someone trusting you to get on with your job and not wanting to interfere.

- Be aware if frustration about rejection is more about your needs than the reality of the situation.

48 FEELING BULLIED

BEING BULLIED OR FEELING BULLIED can have a devastating effect on self-esteem and needs to be faced up to resolutely.

The idea

It is worth thinking about how your requests are received. Setting out clear expectations can be seen as creating demanding pressures that can be tantamount to bullying. Some may say they are being bullied when in fact perfectly reasonable expectations are being put on them. For others the bullying is real, with no understanding by the individual causing the bullying about the effect they are having on the recipient.

Remorseless demands with no regard for resources available turn into bullying when emotional and financial pressures demean people who are seeking to deliver. The word 'bullying' is sometimes used as a way of pushing back when someone feels that expectations are not reasonable. It may be an emotional reaction of exasperation, or an authentic description of what is happening in reality.

If you begin to feel bullied, it is worth dissecting carefully whether the phrase is an accurate description of what is happening or whether it is an emotional reaction to the way you are being treated. Whether the bullying is real or apparent, the feeling of being bullied can create a frustration that wants to push back or shock people into action.

If you are feeling bullied, seek a perspective from trusted others to differentiate between acts of bullying and the perception of bullying.

Seeking the perspective of two or three different people will enable you to decide how best to handle this frustration. Is it something that is a by-product of a particularly stressful time, or is there an undercurrent of inappropriate behaviour that needs to be tackled?

Craig felt 'got at' by his boss because he had not delivered two projects on time. His boss had set out clear expectations and had been willing to talk through what might need to happen in terms of reordering priorities to enable those expectations to be met. Craig recognised that, in this situation, his feeling of being bullied did not match the reality of what was happening.

When Craig moved to a different role and felt that unreasonable expectations were being placed on him, he sought to address this issue with his new boss. This time he met a very different response. The boss's demands became stronger: he was not willing to talk through prioritisation or to countenance a different way of allocating resources. His tone of voice became aggressive, with a deluge of swear words on a couple of occasions. Craig felt that on this occasion he was being bullied. This was a frustration he needed to share with the HR Department, who did not seem surprised when he talked through his concerns with them.

In practice

- When you feel bullied, try to distinguish the emotional reaction of feeling bullied from the experience of being bullied.

- Seek the views of trusted others about how they perceive someone's behaviour.

- Where a boss's behaviour is patently out of line with the values of the organisation, be prepared to refer your concerns to the HR Department.

- If you are frustrated about feeling bullied, the likelihood is that others are being subjected to the same experience.

49 SADNESS

SADNESS CAN LEAD TO calm reflection or inner preoccupation.

The idea

Sadness for a leader can be a consequence of grief when valued colleagues move on. Delight and sadness may occur at the same time when a project has been completed and members of the team move on to other activities. When there is the shock of a tragic death or unexpected health issues, sadness can affect any team acutely. The grief cycle can often take two years. In a work situation it may well be much less than two years, but the length of time taken to move on from sadness should not be underestimated.

Part of handling sadness at work is recognising grief and sadness and not pretending they do not exist. When the government department for which I was the HR Director was merged with another department, I organised a big party for the wider leadership that was no longer going to exist as a separate entity. It was a celebratory 'wake'. Marking the end of the department in this way allowed people to express their sadness and be ready to move on to be part of the new organisation. It was a therapeutic event that allowed grief and sadness to be expressed. The speech I gave was based on the passage in Ecclesiastes that talked of 'a time to tear down and a time to build, a time to weep and a time to laugh, a time to mourn and a time to dance'.

It is important as a leader that we recognise anger and grief in organisations and that we enable people to recognise there is a time to move on and leave the sadness behind. We can be in the grip of sadness one day, and on the following day be frustrated by our own sadness and want to move forward. Moving on from sadness always involves respecting the causes of the sadness. Sadness can also be a corporate emotion, where our role as a leader is about enabling others to work through sadness.

When Martha's team leader retired because of ill-health, Martha knew that she would miss his wisdom. She had not fully appreciated how sad she would feel about his departure. This emotion was exacerbated by the reality that her boss's life was going to be limited because of his cancer. Martha's boss spoke individually to his direct reports, encouraging them to view his successor positively, but Martha found it difficult to immediately warm to his successor.

Martha felt almost overwhelmed by sadness for the two weeks after her boss departed. She slowly became frustrated with her own sadness, but did not know how best to move on. Over time she began to appreciate her new boss while recognising that it would take a while before she could say that she had moved on from the experience of sadness.

In practice

- Accept that changes in your work situation can create a deeper sense of sadness and grief than you might have expected.

- Accept that it takes time to move through the grief cycle.

- Accept that there will be a point where you become frustrated with your own sadness and will need to find ways of coming to terms with your sadness and allow it to gradually diminish.

50 STRESS

STRESS FROM PEOPLE AROUND YOU is contagious. How best do you protect yourself from the adverse consequences of their stress?

The idea

When you are considering joining a team, it can be helpful to ask: how does the team handle stress? Lively dialogue and working through differences is part of the life of any organisation. If everyone thinks the same way there is little chance of constructive forward thinking. Healthy debate and dialogue can quickly turn into stress if the expectations do not match what is possible or if competition begins to have adverse consequences.

When a leader becomes stressed, this rapidly transmits itself to those around them. You can feel enmeshed in the stress of your boss as if you are caught in a net. Sometimes you have to move physically away from the people causing you stress in order to regain your calm.

Sometimes you understand that stress flows from particular events or shocks. The stress in leaders is understandable at these moments and has to be accepted for a period. What is more concerning is when the stress is relentless and has a debilitating effect on everyone around the leader.

Many organisations now have 360-degree feedback exercises where people can, through anonymous means, express concerns about whether or not the leadership approach is creating a positive environment. However, when told that they are creating a stressful environment, some leaders see that as a good thing in order to keep people alert. Others, by contrast, are concerned if they are regarded as leading in a way that is stress-inducing.

Hannah was naturally calm and measured in her approach. She did not raise her voice but had a track record of delivering effective outcomes. She recognised that her new boss had a reputation as someone who was stressful and could be volatile in his reactions to different situations. She was bold enough to ask her boss how she might best respond if he was becoming agitated.

Because Hannah had worked with this individual before, she was not inhibited from posing this question. Her boss was self-aware enough to know exactly why she was asking this question. Their agreement was that whenever Hannah observed her boss becoming over-stressed and agitated, she should feel free to find a moment to point out to him what she saw. Going forward, Hannah felt she would be confident enough to pose this question to any future boss, even if she had not worked with them before.

In practice

- Do due diligence before appointing someone to test whether they exude stress or calmness.

- Do not underestimate how infectious stress can be and be willing to get people to face up to the consequences of their own stress.

- When you begin to feel frustrated about the stress level that others are displaying, be observant about the stress levels that you might be exhibiting.

- Be ready to differentiate between inevitable stress at particular key points and relentless stress that needs to be tackled.

REPUTATION

OUR REPUTATION GOES BEFORE US, whether we like it or not.

The idea

Reputations are inherent in any organisation. You can help promote healthy reputations by commending to one person the contribution of another. The sharing of stories about what has happened in an organisation can create a sense of community and belonging, reinforcing the positive reputation of individuals and teams. The repeating of stories about events that have turned out well can generate laughter and relaxation, as well as building up positive reputations and legacies.

Negative reputations can mean a legacy of suspicion and mistrust. If a colleague is talked of in a critical way, you are likely to assume that you, too, may be the subject of negative remarks. Negative stories being circulated can create caution in individuals, who are less likely to share fully their ideas and perspective.

It is always helpful to know what your reputation is in order to understand how you are perceived. You may be accepting of some aspects of the reputation if it caricatures accurately your approach. When the reputation is about your being supportive or demanding in a fair way, then you might be entirely content with these perceptions.

If, however, you discover that your reputation is for being grumpy on Monday mornings, you might want to think about how you behave so you can dispel the perception that Monday morning is not a good time for people to approach you. It is inevitable that reputations continue for longer than is necessarily deserved. You may have ceased to be grumpy on Monday mornings a few months ago, but stories can still be circulating about your likely reaction on a Monday to requests.

When you feel frustrated on hearing about your reputation, treat the information as valuable data and be deliberate in deciding how you want to respond. Try to be amused by what people say about you rather than being deflated by what you hear.

Michael knew he had a reputation for being five minutes late for meetings. The consequence was that everyone assumed that his meetings would start five minutes late. Michael was flattered that people saw his presence at a meeting as important and recognised that he should not be wasting people's time by being late. He set his watch three minutes early as a technique to try to ensure he was at meetings on time; but he rapidly discounted that three minutes in his mind so that technique did not work.

Michael recognised that he needed to be more disciplined to arrive at meetings three minutes early. He was explicit in saying this was what he was trying to do. Most of his colleagues did not believe that he would keep this resolution and were surprised when he did so. His reputation for always being late for meetings lasted for at least another year.

In practice

- Recognise the inevitability of having a reputation and seek to be amused by it.

- Help build up the positive reputation of those who demonstrate the type of behaviours you want to encourage.

- Take seriously what you hear about your reputation.

- Be deliberate in changing your working practices—and saying why you are changing these practices—when you want your reputation to change.

FEELING LET DOWN

WHEN YOU FEEL LET DOWN, you might become morose and disengaged and need to find ways of moving on.

The idea

You can feel let down when a person you have appointed disappoints or colleagues do not deliver on their commitments. You believe it is important to trust people but have learnt over time the importance of both trusting and triangulating to keep yourself informed about what is happening. You do not want to interfere, partially to protect your own time, but also so that those people you trust believe that they genuinely have the discretion you have given them.

When you feel let down, it might be for good reason. Your peer has had to deal with other, unexpected priorities. Your member of staff might have had unexpected health or family dilemmas to contend with. Rather than allowing yourself to be immediately frustrated by feeling let down, it helps to seek to understand what has been the cause of them holding back from fulfilling their commitments.

When you feel the frustration of being let down, you may want to both blame the individual and yourself for placing your trust in this person. It helps to be philosophical. There will always be situations where you feel let down. The more adventurous you are in giving responsibility to different people or building partnerships with different colleagues, the greater the likelihood of both successful outcomes and of limited progress in some instances.

What matters is seeking to identify a situation early enough where you might feel let down so that you can take steps to address it. The frustration that flows from feeling let down is more readily addressed than some other frustrations caused by others, but may well involve difficult conversations where you have to make your perspective clear and work jointly on next steps.

Rhiannon felt let down by her job-share partner. Rhiannon had worked hard to provide papers for a key meeting that was going to take place when her job-share partner was occupying the role. The feedback Rhiannon received was that her job-share partner had said very little in the meeting and not been influential. Rhiannon had invested a lot in this piece of work. She enjoyed working with her job-share partner most of the time and was not sure how to handle her frustration about this particular incident.

Rhiannon and her partner had a face-to-face stocktake every Wednesday. This provided the opportunity for Rhiannon to ask her partner about her perceptions of what happened at the meeting. Her partner readily confessed that she had not prepared adequately for the meeting and had been disappointed in her own contribution. This sense of remorse helped Rhiannon handle her own frustration. It led to a good conversation about how they would handle similar situations going forward. Rhiannon resolved to prepare her colleague better for subsequent meetings, and her colleague promised that she would put more time into preparing before going into these meetings.

In practice

- Accept the inevitability that you will feel let down from time to time.

- Seek to identify the underlying causes of what has gone wrong.

- Try to avoid jumping to negative conclusions about the lack of commitment from others.

- Believe this is a frustration that should be temporary and can be addressed quickly.

DISCRIMINATION

THE FRUSTRATION CAUSED by discrimination can be acutely emotive.

The idea

A solicitor who is black told me that his clients who are black preferred to appear before a judge from the same racial group as themselves on the basis that they were less likely to be discriminated against. This solicitor told his clients that a judge who was black could well give a tougher sentence to someone from a similar ethnic background, as the judge might feel that the person being tried had let their shared ethnic group down.

Discrimination in the sense of treating people less fairly than others is complex, as it may occur as much within similar groups as between members of different groups based on gender, ethnicity, cultural background, age or sexuality.

When you feel frustrated because of apparent discrimination, saying you feel discriminated against can be counter-productive. Colleagues you work with might immediately become more wary of how they engage with you and be less willing to be open and trusting. When discrimination and unfairness has occurred, pursuing a formal complaint must be right. But an accusation of discrimination can sometimes be, and seem to be, an overreaction to inevitable friction and misunderstandings that can happen within any organisation.

If you feel frustration caused by discrimination, it is worth checking with trusted others about whether they think that deliberate or institutional discrimination is happening. Where events happen that might be construed as discrimination, an early conversation can help cast light on the reasons for this and what might be the best ways forward.

Shirley was a black lesbian who talked openly about her recent marriage. When her boss gave the lead on an interesting project to her colleague, part of Shirley's inner reaction was to think she might have been discriminated against. Her boss was a white male who was heavily involved in a church that did not approve of gay marriage. Shirley felt a growing sense of frustration about whether her boss had discriminated against her.

Rather than let this perception fester, Shirley decided she should have a conversation with her boss to ask for his reasons for passing the project to her colleague. His reasons were cogent. Shirley took a different opportunity to ask her boss what his perspective was on the fact that she was a lesbian. Shirley was pleasantly surprised by her boss's reaction as he said he was fully supportive of gay people becoming married in civil ceremonies. The fact that Shirley and her boss were able to have an open conversation about this subject reassured Shirley that no discrimination had been intended.

In practice

- Be wary if your immediate reaction is to assume that you are being discriminated against.

- Seek to understand why decisions have been made before presuming that discrimination has happened.

- Be willing to talk openly with those who you think might be treating you unfairly in order to understand their perspective.

- Be doubly conscious about how you treat others so that you cannot be reasonably accused of being discriminatory in your practices.

PREJUDICE

PREJUDICE CAUSES PAINFUL FRUSTRATION, which might mean moving on to a different role.

The idea

When I joined the UK Civil Service in 1972, I had the perception that the system was prejudiced in favour of graduates from public schools who had been to Oxford and Cambridge universities. I was a northerner who went to a local school and a northern university. The posh voices of some of my new colleagues tended to reinforce this perception. Those males with loud, posh voices seemed to be able to make their presence felt more easily in meetings and, therefore, seemed to be listened to more readily than I was. I developed a sense of frustration that was at risk of holding me back.

I soon realised that the problem was far more about my own perceptions. Perhaps I was prejudiced against those who had come from a different background to me. Any sense that the system favoured people from a posh background was soon dispelled, but I had to eradicate my own prejudice.

A few years later, a Secretary of State I worked closely with gave me a severe talking-to, saying that I was now on track to being a senior member of the civil service and should stop feeling I was 'only a lad from Yorkshire' and eradicate any sense of prejudice I had about people from a posh background.

When we feel the frustration of prejudice because others are being favoured, it can be enlightening to reflect on the prejudices we bring and how they frustrate us. Being honest with ourselves about our own prejudices and seeking to be amused by the apparent prejudices of others can help us deal more lightly with these frustrations.

Henry was making good progress within the architectural practice he had joined a few years earlier. He noticed that all the senior people in the practice had studied at Sheffield University. They got on well and thought in similar ways. Henry had studied at Leeds Metropolitan University, which was a former polytechnic. He suspected that his senior colleagues might be a bit snooty about the fact that he had studied at a lower-tier university. His colleagues kept talking about alumni events at Sheffield University, which fuelled his suspicions about possible prejudice.

Henry made sure that he kept up to speed with the thinking coming out of the Leeds Metropolitan University Architecture Department. He brought in some examples of thought leadership from this department, which were well received by his colleagues. He soon concluded that any feeling of prejudice about the architectural school at which he had studied was in his own mind. Henry had found a way of addressing this feeling of prejudice and could dismiss the frustration as unfounded.

In practice

- Be honest with yourself about which categories of people you might be prejudiced against.

- Beware lest apparent 'club think' by colleagues causes you unnecessary angst.

- Where there is unnecessary stereotyping, be willing to speak about it and help change people's perceptions.

- Accept that much of the frustration that comes from prejudice is unfounded.

- Recognise that when prejudice is substantive and persistent, it needs to be addressed.

55 | AGEISM

THE FRUSTRATION CAUSED BY ageism is often in our own minds rather than in the minds of others.

The idea

One of the healthy aspects of the current era is that age is much less of a consideration. Competence and attitude matter more than age. Flight attendants now vary widely in age and are more representative of the population they are serving.

I am still working the equivalent of full-time as I approach the age of 70. I encourage people to think that 70 is the new 50. But ageism can still be a problem when a group of people of a particular age prefer working with those of a similar generation. This preference can apply just as much to people in their 60s as to people in their 30s. It is the responsibility of any leader to ensure that ageism does not take hold within the leadership group.

Recognising the value of bringing a diversity of ages together means drawing on a mixture of wisdom and experience, alongside a sense of curiosity and adventure. Often, older people are more willing to be creative because they are more financially secure than some of their younger colleagues. Some of the brighter younger people may be much more risk-averse because they are conscious that they have dependents and significant financial commitments and do not want to risk losing their employment.

If you begin to feel frustrated because of the age of those around you, it is worth thinking about the reasons for this frustration. You might feel you have less energy than your colleagues, but you bring greater experience. You might feel that you do not have the breadth of understanding of your colleagues, but you bring a fresh, creative and open mind.

Whatever our age, we might feel that we suffer more frustrations than people of a different age. But the frustrations are different rather than greater. For those in their 30s, it may be the frustration of looking after children whose sleep pattern is unpredictable. For those in their 50s, it might be the draining effect of caring for parents with dementia.

Frank sometimes felt that the younger members of his project team were not taking him seriously. They were much more adept in using IT than he was. When he felt frustrated by his inability to keep up with his colleagues, he had to remind himself that his younger colleagues often came to him to seek advice. He was able to help them think through issues and bring a more level-headed approach than they might have done had they not been able to draw on his advice and long experience.

Frank recognised that he would have to live with an element of frustration resulting from the greater technical abilities of his colleagues, but he also saw how he could help reduce the frustration of his colleagues by helping them bring a more structured approach to working through complicated issues.

In practice

- Recognise the benefits that flow from each decade in your life.

- Let the frustrations that flow from the preoccupations of your particular age sit lightly on you.

- See a mixture of ages as making a key contribution to effective teams.

- Seek to be amused by the frustrations that affect your particular age group.

- Be ready to speak out if there are risks of different age groups being treated more favourably than others.

56 FAVOURITISM TO OTHERS

WHEN YOU ARE NOT ASKED to take on a particular role, an easy excuse is to say to yourself that favouritism has been shown to someone else.

The idea

We believe that people should be appointed on merit. At the same time, we recognise that a team leader may want to appoint a mix of people who bring different sets of expertise and experience. The team leader will be looking at the individual merits of one person, as well as the overall skillset they want to build in a team. What might appear as favouritism could reflect a deliberate choice to appoint a candidate who brings a distinctive set of skills needed for the team to be successful.

There are moments when you might have been the right person at the right time. It might have felt to others that you had benefited from favouritism. In my first career in the UK Government, there were times when I had been the right person at the right time, for example, when I was appointed as Press Secretary to the Secretary of State. But when his successor was appointed, this new Secretary of State wanted to bring with him his previous press secretary, so I was the wrong person at the wrong time on that occasion.

One way of handling the frustration of apparent favouritism to others is to accept that a decision might go in your favour on some occasions and in favour of someone else at other times. Recognising the inevitability that leaders will want to build their own teams can help engender an acceptance of the reality that appointments are rarely made purely on individual merit.

If a category of people is always favoured within an organisation, it is right to express concern, perhaps initially as a question rather than a protest. A well-put question about how best an organisation can ensure fairness in the allocation of responsibilities and promotions can prompt a proper debate and send a warning shot across the bow of any leaders who are considering favouring particular categories of people. The biggest danger is people favouring those who are like them and rejecting the notion that teams can be at their most effective when they include a mix of people with different credentials.

As HR Manager, Jacqui was concerned that one director kept appointing people who he had previously worked with. He seemed to be reluctant to appoint people he did not know. Jacqui had a conversation with the director where she asked him how he thought others in the organisation would view his decisions. He was surprised by Jacqui's concern and quickly saw that there was a potential perception problem with his decisions.

This gentle prodding from Jacqui helped the director recognise that there was an underlying favouritism that he was not fully acknowledging. He was then deliberate in ensuring that the next appointments to his team were not people he had worked with before. Jacqui had turned her frustration from observing the director's decisions into a constructive conversation that had brought home to him how these decisions could be interpreted.

In practice

- Be mindful about how decisions could appear to indicate favouritism towards a particular type of candidate.

- When you become frustrated by the apparent favouritism of others, recognise that you might be inadvertently behaving the same way.

- When you observe someone who looks as if they are acting favourably to particular categories of people, try asking a few innocent questions rather than going for a direct approach.

57 MIXED MESSAGES

MIXED MESSAGES CAN INADVERTENTLY create confusion and unnecessary frustration.

The idea

Two people in positions of responsibility may give messages that are not entirely consistent. Their respective recollections of a meeting may be slightly different. How they relay decisions may be influenced by their own preferences and approaches. When messages are not entirely consistent, our reactions can be a mix of frustration, concern and curiosity.

Frustrations flow when we feel a lack of clarity because mixed messages are holding us back from moving forwards. If we can retain a sense of curiosity, we will have a reason to explore why we have heard two different messages. Is it because one person has understood more clearly what the conclusions were, or was there a mix of conclusions, with both accounts being correct, even if they are not entirely consistent?

When a pair of instructions are inconsistent, there is a choice to be made about whether you take whatever action you think is appropriate in the light of conflicting advice or seek more clarity before you act.

When there are mixed messages, frustration can be unhelpful and can mean you build up an issue into something bigger than it is. Try to hold the frustration at bay until you have found out more about what happened. In many cases, the mixed messages are a result of misunderstandings rather than a deliberate attempt to confuse.

There are occasions when two people are quite deliberately setting out their preferred courses of action and are cognisant that there is a degree of contradiction. It is a perfectly reasonable for you to request clarity and to expect the two principals to agree a way forward.

Edward worked closely with a Minister of State in a government department who gave regular messages about the importance of a particular review. Edward also heard from the private secretary to the Secretary of State that this review was not high up the Secretary of State's personal agenda. Edward recognised such mixed messaging was part of the life of a civil servant when a junior minister was ambitiously seeking to build a reputation for themselves, whereas the Secretary of State held a more dispassionate view across a wider spectrum of responsibility.

Edward gently asked the Minister of State whether he had the full support of the Secretary of State. The Minister immediately said yes. Edward risked asking the Minister of State when he had last spoken to the Secretary of State on this subject. At that point the Minister went quiet. Edward did not press his concern, but noted that in his next conversation, the Minister volunteered that he had recently spoken with the Secretary of State and got his approval for a particular timescale. Edward took the precaution of asking the Secretary of State's private secretary if this was an accurate description of the Secretary of State's view and received a rather grudging, lukewarm response. This gave Edward enough of a steer to decide to give this piece of work reasonable priority, but not the highest priority.

In practice

- Be curious when you hear mixed messages, rather than becoming frustrated.

- See mixed messages as inevitable and only sometimes deliberate.

- Choose your moment to push back when you are having to interpret mixed messages.

- Don't expect absolute consistency in the messages you receive.

58 BROKEN PROMISES

BROKEN PROMISES ARE a fact of life. We have to accept them and move on.

The idea

When a marriage ends, the initial promises made when two people got married have been terminated. Some would describe this as an example of broken promises, others would regard it as the ending of a contract which has not stood the test of time. It is often said that a promise is only as good as the piece of paper it is written on. Promises become overtaken by events. People and situations change. A promise to deliver on a contract or agreement is no guarantee that it will be fulfilled.

Life is littered with broken promises. We can choose to get frustrated on a weekly basis by commitments that we feel have been broken. Perhaps we have to tell ourselves that we need to 'get over it' and move on. It is not always as easy as giving ourselves a straight talking and moving on, but we do ourselves no good by churning over in our minds frustrations caused by broken promises.

When we agree contracts with different parties, it involves a commitment to deliver on a particular timescale. Sometimes it can be worth pressing a partner about how committed they are to fulfilling the terms of a contract by asking them, 'Are you promising to deliver as in this contract?' If your interlocutor is hesitant about responding, then you might feel justified in being frustrated about their intent to deliver.

I am conscious that there are a small number of people with whom I have entered into an understanding or contract and have delivered services for them and they have failed to pay the invoice. You sometimes reach the stage where it is not worth the effort of trying to force them to pay. Continued effort has become pointless and you have to move on. But a broken promise is still a broken promise, and their reputation in your mind is forever tarnished.

Roseanne was leading a building project with a tight timescale. She needed some engineering work done at a particular time in the process for the overall project to be completed on schedule. Her chosen contractor had said the timescale was feasible. When Roseanne pressed the contractor about his promise to deliver, she was given an unequivocal affirmative response. But when the time came for the engineer's work to begin, he began to make excuses about delay with a previous piece of work.

Roseanne became suspicious and confronted him about when the work was going to be done. She felt there was a risk that she was being taken advantage of as a woman. She decided that she needed to be deliberate in her language about giving the engineer a last opportunity to fulfil their commitment. At the same time, Roseanne was making contingent enquiries about using an alternative firm and was directing her frustration into finding a suitable alternative way forward. She recognised that she needed to be decisive in standing down the first contractor. They had agreed at the contract stage very clear timescales so the contractor could not legitimately accuse her of breaking the contract.

In practice

- `Accept that promises get broken and try not to get too upset when that happens.

- Keep a careful watch for when promises are at risk of being broken and do contingency planning.

- Observe any growing frustration in you about whether a contractual commitment is likely to be broken and use this as early warning to test out what is happening.

59 CHANGED ASSUMPTIONS

WHEN ASSUMPTIONS KEEP CHANGING outside your control, allow yourself to indulge in short-term frustration—then regroup, reframe and move on.

The idea

When I led on a major piece of reorganisation within a government department, it was at the specific request of a newly appointed Permanent Secretary. The assumption was that he would be in post for the long term, which was why he wanted to fundamentally restructure the department. To my surprise, after a few weeks he told me he had been appointed as the Vice Chancellor of a university; he acknowledged that I might be taken aback by his decision.

I recognised that his successor might take a very different view about the future. I sought to keep up the momentum on the project I was leading, but knew it was unlikely to have the same impetus. The new Permanent Secretary wanted to take a more limited approach, so that certain aspects of the project's recommendations were implemented and others discarded. I was surprised by how calm I was by this shift in circumstances. Working for a sequence of ministers from different political parties had taught me that assumptions can change rapidly and the priority of one day can become the irrelevance of the next day.

For those who have been involved in a long-term project or programme, a changed assumption can feel like a devastating blow. Your life's work looks as if it is being questioned, but new sponsors or funders have every right to reassess assumptions and decide that the strategy for one season is not right for the next period. Assumptions come and go, and we have to live with changing assumptions and not get too hung up when a new administration or leadership describes success in an entirely different way. We might need to allow ourselves half-hour bursts of frustration, and then seek to get on with the task in hand.

Laura had a senior post in a supermarket chain, where the focus had been on developing megastores. The priority then shifted away from megastores to numerous smaller stores with a more local clientele. She had been recruited with the prospectus of being part of the design team for the next generation of bigger stores, which had excited her creative instincts.

When the change of store policy was announced with an embargo on new, big stores, she felt intensely disappointed. She was not interested in design work on glorified corner shops, but she knew she had to overcome her annoyance. For perfectly good reasons the business had changed its strategy.

Laura had to go with that change in strategy or leave. There was no point in a grudging acceptance of a new strategy. She had to wholeheartedly shift the focus of her design work and accept the policy, or seek to join an organisation that was still in the business of megastores. She concluded that a couple of long walks with a good friend were needed before she could decide what to do next.

In practice

- Accept that business assumptions change at an ever-faster pace.

- Develop a mindset that recognises that assumptions will inevitably keep changing.

- See the upside of ever-changing assumptions as being that there will be new opportunities that are currently unforeseen.

60 | BEING MISREPRESENTED

BEING MISREPRESENTED CAN MAKE you feel cross, with deliberate action being necessary.

The idea

Colleagues may make assumptions about why you have taken certain decisions and articulate what they perceive as your perspective. Any leader is at risk of their innocent comments being turned into major pronouncements. They then feel misrepresented, when all someone has done is build a scenario out of one or two remarks. They may well have thought they were doing the right thing in interpreting your comments in a particular way. They were not trying to misrepresent you, even though the effect of them extrapolating your views had been to misrepresent you.

On other occasions a misrepresentation might be deliberate. Critics may well want to damage your credibility by misrepresenting your views and seek to create dissonance. The technique of representing a view in an extreme way is increasingly deployed by users of social media—many people assume that whatever is said on social media is therefore a misrepresentation of the truth.

When you feel misrepresented, the positive is that someone feels your view is significant enough to seek to distort. You may not want to respond in haste and regret at leisure if there is a danger that you respond in a needlessly aggressive way to a misrepresentation of your viewpoint. It is worth reflecting calmly on your position so that you express it clearly and through appropriate channels in seeking to counter misrepresentation. It is likely to involve choosing your moment carefully and deciding which aspects of misrepresentation need to be countered and which you can let pass by.

As Finance Director, Louise set out the reasons why a particular initiative could not be funded. She was careful not to dismiss the idea out of hand and wanted to set out the evidence she would need to be supportive of the project in the future. Her views were reported back in a very casual way to the project leader, with the message implying that Louise had dismissed the idea out of hand without giving it careful consideration. Unsurprisingly, the director of the project was disgruntled.

When Louise heard about how her views had been described, she felt that she had been misrepresented. She had said 'no', but she had been clear what needed to happen for her to reconsider her approach. Louise did not want her own or the project director's frustration to fester. Louise phoned her colleague and set out in clear terms what she had said to the messenger who had apparently misrepresented her view. Through this early, open conversation, the frustration of being misrepresented was dissipated.

In practice

- Accept that you are likely to be misrepresented on a regular basis.

- Set out your reasons clearly so that the chances of being misrepresented are reduced.

- When there is evidence of misrepresentation, decide on how this is best addressed expeditiously, and in a measured and not emotive way.

61 | AN OUTDATED REPUTATION

Our reputation lives on long after the events that shaped it have passed.

The idea

Others will associate triumphs or debacles with us many years after they have occurred. Your name may be linked with a particularly successful project, or you may be associated with a particular reverse. Both types of reputations have a downside. You want to be known for what you are contributing now rather than what you contributed 10 or 20 years ago. You may have learnt a lot from a programme that was not regarded as successful and become a more effective leader because of your experience of living through a failure.

When your reputation is broadly positive, the main frustration flows from others not fully appreciating the contribution you can bring now and the way your skills and experience have further developed. If you are linked with something that did not go well, you can turn that experience into a virtue and articulate clearly what you have learnt from past events.

What is key is how you can present past experience in a convincing and positive way. You don't have to try to persuade people that you got it right when you got it wrong. You will be more convincing if you can present a coherent story about your learning.

If there is an area where your reputation is not as strong as you would like it to be, it is worth addressing that situation. If you are not regarded as a good public speaker, investing in your public speaking skills is not going to be wasted. You might volunteer to speak at a range of different types of events and try different approaches. The more you can deploy your skills in situations where you do not feel entirely comfortable, the more confident you will be in demonstrating your effectiveness in challenging situations.

Richard had a reputation for talking too much and not listening well. Over the years, he had recognised this feedback and deliberately tried to listen more and talk less. He maintained his resolve most of the time, but in stressful situations he tended to revert to type and produce a deluge of words.

When he was at risk of talking too much, Richard would hold a glass of water and drink it slowly. He would ration himself in a conversation to three points and no more. He would be deliberate in asking the views of others and stop himself from responding immediately to things with which he did not fully agree. He would often ask a colleague to sum up at the end of a meeting so that the voice that was in people's mind when they left was not his.

Richard felt he had taken all the right steps, but he was disappointed that there had been limited progress in terms of his reputation. When Richard lost his voice temporarily, he was teased about it. As his voice gradually recovered, he recognised that he had to ration his interventions so that his voice was restored gradually. This proved to be a superb way of disciplining and moderating his interventions.

In practice

- Accept that reputations live on for a long time.

- Recognise the positives about your reputation that you can build on.

- Be deliberate in addressing the more negative aspects of your reputation by being explicit in saying how you have addressed these concerns.

- On the basis that reputations come and go, do not get overly frustrated if you have a negative reputation about some aspects of your approach.

62 LACK OF ALIGNMENT

A LACK OF ALIGNMENT causes immense frustration to those observing a 'dialogue of the deaf'.

The idea

During 2018, it was frustrating to watch the lack of alignment between the EU and UK negotiators on Brexit. For months there appeared to be a dialogue between two sides not hearing each other. A neutral observer might have questioned whether both parties wanted to find a constructive way forward. An alignment of intent was essential for progress, but shouting from the barricades was the recurring impression.

Where there is a lack of genuine alignment, joint endeavours are unlikely to move forward. True alignment involves building a shared prospectus about outcomes and a strong sense of partnership. Progress is most likely when there are aligned next steps that can be to the benefit of all parties.

When you are frustrated about a lack of alignment, frank conversations may be necessary. Sticking to the purity of an initial intent and not being open to being pragmatic makes the lack of alignment even more acute. Addressing a lack of alignment involves the hard work of building trust and seeking to negotiate a constructive way forward. It means a shared prospectus with your so-called supporters as much as with those you are negotiating with.

Often you have to accept that misalignment is a fact of life. The staff association and the management are unlikely to have completely aligned objectives. But both parties will be conscious that if there can be areas where they are aligned, then the chances of handling issues with mutual understanding is much increased.

Susan did not feel at all aligned with the union officials with whom she had to discuss closing some branch offices. The union official was even more frustrated than she was, as he felt she held the trump cards. He knew that Susan's room for manoeuvre was limited, but he was not going to make it easy for her. He recognised that some offices were going to be closed, but he was going to make a fuss about this because he wanted to demonstrate that he was a tough union official.

Susan recognised that this misalignment was not going to disappear. She set out clearly how the redundancies were going to be handled in a fair and reasoned way. She was not expecting endorsement from the union official. The most she was going to get was grudging acquiescence. Susan recognised that she would have to accept the union official's dismissive language and not let it frustrate her too much. She was patient with him and always personally considerate. She did not rise to the bait when he taunted her or when his language became intemperate. She had been through similar negotiations before and recognised that she had to keep her cool, whatever her level of personal frustration.

In practice

- Seek to reduce the amount of misalignment, recognising that you might be able to diminish it but not remove it.

- Accept that a lack of alignment is inevitable while seeking to build stronger levels of mutual understanding.

- Seek to see issues from the perspective of sceptics and critics in order to gain insight about how misalignment is being fuelled.

BEING IGNORED

BEING IGNORED FEELS FAR worse than disagreement or criticism.

The idea

Have you ever fallen into the habit of ignoring someone? They have taken up more of your energy than you can afford to give. Their priorities may be different from yours, with the consequence that you feel disoriented talking to them. Perhaps they exude a disapproval of what you do and how you engage with others. You want to avoid them and pretend they are not there—hence you blank them out. Once you begin to ignore someone, you get into a pattern of not needing or wanting to talk to them and they cease to exist in your mind.

If there is a risk that you might adopt that approach to someone who is annoying you, might someone else adopt that approach towards you? If you feel you are being deliberately ignored, it is worth first checking with colleagues whether they think your perception is accurate. It may be that they are feeling ignored too; or they may comment that the person you are concerned about is so absorbed in their responsibilities that they are ignoring certain people to focus on current priorities.

The negative effect you can have on others when you do ignore them should be a wake-up call. Hence the importance of offering at least a smile or a nod in their direction when you are preoccupied with business that you currently judge to be of greater significance.

You will want to assess whether the sense of being ignored is a short- or long-term issue. If it seems persistent, there has to be a point when you talk your concerns through with the individual, with a discussion about how best you might both move on. A frustration about being ignored that festers can damage a perfectly reasonable working relationship.

Nick felt that his boss did not take much notice of him. Nick was quiet and did not readily speak with his boss. Most of the team were reserved and the boss focused on his computer screen rather than his colleagues. Nick felt he was not appreciated by his boss because his boss hardly ever spoke to him. This distance between him and his boss became a big issue for Nick and began to affect his self-confidence.

There was a breakthrough when there was a team coaching event and each member of the team talked about their preferred ways of working. Nick began to appreciate that his boss was naturally very reserved and did not volunteer conversation with others, while at the same time he was supportive of his staff. His boss made some positive comments about Nick's contribution that greatly encouraged him. He felt he could leave behind his perception of feeling ignored by his boss once he knew and understood more about how his boss naturally interacted with colleagues.

In practice

- Beware lest you overreact when feeling ignored.

- Be mindful that you might appear to be ignoring others.

- Triangulate with colleagues whether they are also feeling ignored.

- If the sense of being ignored continues, seek an opportunity to talk it through with your colleague.

64 LOSING YOUR JOB

THOSE AROUND YOU WILL be watching carefully to see how you respond when you lose your job and how you handle your frustration.

The idea

I have lost my job on four occasions and on three of them I did not see the situation coming. What kept me going was the belief that good can come out of any situation: the seed has to die before there can be new life. On each occasion there was initially a numbness followed by a combination of frustration and a determination to move on constructively.

I now see each event as a defining moment that led to good outcomes over time. In retrospect I am so relieved that I did not let a sense of frustration get the better of me. I sought to direct the inevitable frustration into positive action about what avenues might open up and how I could direct my attention in a constructive way. Looking back, I could so easily have let frustration turn into resentment, which it did for a period in one of the times. I was saved from this sinking into resentment by a combination of support from my family, mentoring from good friends and a faith perspective which holds that there can be new life and hope in the most difficult of situations.

Losing your job can be a long-drawn-out process or it can happen in an instant. Your organisation is taken over and redundancies are announced—you have to live with this reality, whether you like it or not. You may feel demeaned, abused, rejected and cast aside.

Frustration wants to burst out of you, but you have to accept that you are the victim of circumstances; you are forced to reassess your thinking about work and life. You are jolted into thinking about what work you want to do next, and consider if this is the moment to change course. For many people the abolition of their current role forces them to embark in a new direction—they then look back on the moment of rejection as a time when new possibilities came into view.

Zara was shocked when her school was closed. She had taught there for five years and had developed a good routine. She went through feelings of disappointment, rejection and despair. A good friend pressed her about what might now be possible which had not been an option before. Zara had enjoyed doing some private tuition and began to think about building this up alongside supply teaching. She began to accept that this could provide her with far greater flexibility than she had previously experienced.

Her question was: could she turn her frustration into exploring an alternative way of using her time and energy? She was jolted into action after her last day at the school because she did not want to be sitting around at home without engaging with children. It was her passion for watching young people grow in knowledge and understanding that enabled her to think positively about a new type of career.

In practice

- Accept that most people will lose their jobs at some point in their working lives—you are not alone when this happens to you.

- See losing your job as a cathartic experience that might open up a very different way forward.

- Seek to turn the frustration you felt when you lost your job into energetically exploring different options.

- Recognise that it takes time before different possibilities can be shaped into serious options.

65 CONTINUOUS CRITICISM

Continuous criticism eats away at our soul and can lead to addictions that damage our mental health.

The idea

How best do you receive criticism? For most people, criticism is received constructively if it is wrapped within genuine affirmation. When criticism is presented in terms of encouraging positive development in knowledge and confidence, then it is received as a positive input and not as destructive and dangerous indictment of our qualities.

When an individual constantly criticises colleagues, it often says more about them than it does about the people they are criticising. The constant critic is unlikely to be comfortable in themselves as a leader. They are often projecting their frustration and disappointment on others. They can become relentless in pressurising their staff and colleagues, without realising the damaging consequences that relentless criticism can have.

Those who have worked for unrelentingly critical bosses have developed their own way of handling the comments. Many learn how to tune out when the boss goes into critical mode. They know when to get out of the way and when not to put a difficult decision to the critical boss. What is inevitable is that when a team has a hypercritical boss, it will not be as effective as it could be.

When a boss is consistently critical, the team may well need to take collective action, presenting their concerns jointly to a higher boss.

Good governance procedures will allow for expressions of discontent to be heard in a dispassionate way so that inappropriate behaviour can be addressed. The demanding boss who is consistently critical can easily fall into an over-directive or even bullying mode. There are times when it is important to use the energy generated by your frustration to speak truth to power.

Edna ran the private office of a chief executive who was perpetually critical. She had become immune to his criticism; however, those who had limited contact with him were shocked when they were met with a string of critical comments. Edna saw part of her role as enabling people to handle her boss's critical comments and to recognise the substantive points in order to determine next steps.

Edna would sometimes let her frustration show with her boss. He was very dependent on Edna and, therefore, would listen when she said to him that his hypercritical tone was being counter-productive. The problem was that he would listen for a while and say that he would change his ways, but rapidly returned to his normal pattern. It was only when Edna said that she could not take his behaviour for much longer that he began to try to adjust his attitude, because he knew how much he depended on Edna to organise his working life.

In practice

- Observe how those who work closely with people who are consistently critical handle their reactions and their frustration.

- Accept that a degree of immunity to criticism is helpful, provided you can recognise nuggets of truth in that criticism.

- Be willing to give feedback to people who are over-critical when you observe how criticism creates counter-productive frustration amongst staff.

SECTION I
HANDLING FRUSTRATIONS
WITH SPECIFIC PEOPLE

YOUR BOSS

YOUR BOSS CANNOT BE IGNORED. You have to deal with your frustrations in relation to your boss.

The idea

Your boss might frustrate you because of the approach they bring. You may feel that they should give you more time and consideration. You may think that they ought to take a deep interest in your area because it is such a high priority, but your boss may see your area as just part of a wider set of responsibilities. They may be giving you less time than you would ideally like because other areas are taking precedence and they are trusting you to get on with your job without needing much intervention from them.

When you feel frustrated that your boss is not giving you enough attention, it is worth standing back to think about why that is happening. It could be for good reason, as they are fully supportive of what you are doing; or it could be they are avoiding you and your area because they find it difficult to see how they can add value.

When you feel frustrated about your boss, it is worth asking yourself whether the causes of this frustration are more about your attitudes than about the approach of your boss. Your need for affirmation or direction may be greater than your boss thinks is necessary. Self-inflicted frustration can be a consequence of you having expectations of what your boss can contribute—expectations that are not the same as his.

It is worth being clear in your own mind what you most need from your boss to help you address any frustration you have about the working relationship. When you are clear which two or three practical steps would help, it can be worth talking these through with your boss to see if you are aligned on next steps.

Jane felt that her boss was dismissive of her and kept ignoring her. Consequently, whenever she met with him, she felt emotional and tended to withdraw and look morose. A colleague asked her why she looked as if she was shrivelling up whenever her boss was in the same vicinity. The colleague invited her to reflect on whether her expectations of her boss were unrealistic. She asked Jane to think through the variety of expectations on her boss and observe how she was handling them.

Jane's colleague suggested that she identify a topic on which she could share some recent data with her boss and have an interesting conversation about the data. She suggested that Jane identify three clear points she wanted to share. In the resulting 15-minute conversation, Jane held her anxiety at bay and explained these three points briefly, which went down well with her boss. The conversation ended with both individuals smiling broadly at each other. There had been a breakthrough, with Jane realising that she should not be so frustrated with her boss in the future.

In practice

- Recognise the variety of pressures on your boss.

- When you feel frustrated with your boss, reflect on whether or not there is justification for this frustration.

- Reflect on how much of your frustration with your boss is because you have unrealistic expectations.

- Think about what practical steps you can take to continue building a good working relationship with your boss.

67 ● SENIOR LEADERSHIP

IT IS WORTH THINKING through who amongst the senior leadership
has an interest in your areas of responsibility and then building a
relationship with them based on this understanding.

The idea

We can view the senior leadership in an organisation as distant and
irrelevant. We can think cynically that they are earning more money
than we do to sit in meetings rather than doing proper work. A touch
of cynicism can lead to either dismissing what they say or ignoring
them—but there can be a moment when the involvement and support
of senior leadership is essential.

We may think that the Finance Head is stuck in his or her own world,
but there will be occasions when we want the Finance Department to
fully understand our concerns. We may think that someone dealing
with strategy or policy is too far away from the operational demands
of the workplace, but there may be times when it would be helpful to
know what forward thinking is being done so that we can input our
ideas and identify potential risks and consequences.

We may feel an underlying frustration that senior leadership is not
being helpful to us. It can be helpful to understand what issues
they are focusing on and the type of considerations that are most
important to them. Having an awareness about the issues that the
senior leadership are addressing helps us keep calm rather than
being annoyed by the apparent irrelevance of what they are saying.
Fostering good communications with senior leadership through
sharing what is likely to be of interest to them will help you reduce

any sense of frustration and create a greater likelihood that the senior leadership will respond positively to you.

Jane felt frustrated with the Finance Head, who always looked busy and preoccupied. She tended to see him as an irrelevance—when he spoke, she did not fully understand what he was saying. His complicated sentences set off a frustrated reaction in Jane that inhibited her from listening to the points he was making.

When a complicated financial issue arose in her area, Jane wanted to solve the problem herself. She got increasingly annoyed that she could not get the right people in the room together. Reluctantly, and in a mood of desperation, she went to see the Finance Head. She was surprised by the undivided attention he gave her. He made a couple of phone calls and the problem was resolved. This was a timely reminder to Jane that the Finance Head was there for a reason and could unblock things that had become stuck.

If she got frustrated with the Finance Head again, Jane reminded herself that he had been a helpful colleague who happened to be very busy and whose demeanour was not always as warm and engaging as she would like.

In practice

- Be open to talking to senior leadership when you have a problem that they can help you solve.

- Recognise the variety of pressures on senior leaders and do not expect them to be especially interested in what you are doing.

- Use short conversations with senior leaders in a planned way to build constructive working relationships for the future.

COLLEAGUES

YOUR COLLEAGUES CAN BE your strongest allies or your most dangerous enemies.

The idea

When two people have worked together as colleagues over a long period, they can be hugely supportive of each other, always believing that the other person's suggestions are right. There can be a resulting risk of groupthink, with a mutual reinforcing of each other's preferences and prejudices. When you have worked with someone for a while, there can be a degree of frustration that they are always nice to you and do not tell you the truth. They always want to be supportive and, therefore, do not want to be critical.

It can be perfectly reasonable to say to a colleague that you are frustrated that they never give you feedback that makes you consider your approach. Hence the importance of inviting colleagues to be frank with you when they think you are going in the wrong direction. You can say that you will be frustrated with them if they do not give you truthful, frank feedback.

The opposite risk is that you become frustrated with colleagues who regularly disagree with you or always look as if they are disapproving of what you are saying. You are anticipating a critical response from them, and may expect negativity when none was intended.

The worst type of group behaviour flows from underlying disapproval of colleagues, which leads to frustration, resentment and unwarranted behaviours. Underlying frustrations with colleagues in a leadership team can fester, with members always entering the room in a negative frame of mind. Team coaching often needs to start with exploring the underlying frustrations between team members. Once these frustrations are named and discussed openly, there can often be a breakthrough.

Jane felt her colleagues were a mixed bunch with whom she did not feel entirely comfortable. She had worked closely with a couple of them over a number of years—they were very comfortable together, but were at risk of looking backwards rather than forwards. There were times when she was frustrated with this nostalgia and felt they could build a much more constructive focus on future development.

Jane found a couple of other colleagues difficult and did not want to engage with them. On one occasion she needed to talk with one of these colleagues prior to a meeting and build a shared approach about how to address a particular issue. Jane observed that in the team meeting she was much more accepting of her colleague's contribution, as they had talked through their different perspectives in advance and had agreed a shared strategy. This was a valuable prompt to Jane, which reminded her she should collaborate with colleagues in advance of meetings.

In practice

- Be aware of the risk of being too comfortable with colleagues you have known a long time so that you avoid facing difficult issues effectively.

- How best might you work on a particular issue with a colleague you find difficult or have an emotional reaction against?

- What type of team coaching or sharing would help surface frustrations between colleagues that need to be addressed?

YOUR STAFF

WHEN YOUR STAFF CAUSE you frustration, you cannot ignore that emotion and have to deal with it.

The idea

When you have an emotional reaction to one of your staff, it is telling you something about the relationship and something about you. A good starting point is asking yourself why you feel frustrated with this person. Does the problem come from your expectations or from the approach and actions of the individual?

The key to understanding this situation is to bring as much objectivity as possible about what is causing the frustration. Does the problem stem from what the staff member is doing or how they are doing it, or the time they are taking to finish particular activities? The question then becomes whether there is a shared understanding between you and this person about of what needs to be done and by when.

Fairness dictates that when someone is causing you frustration, there is an open conversation about why this is happening. Good practice suggests there needs to be agreement about a mutually understood approach going forward, covering the key considerations about what could be done, how it is to be achieved and by when.

When you are frustrated by a member of your staff, it is worth remembering that they are likely to be equally frustrated with you. Understanding why you cause them frustration provides insight about how best you can work together going forward, minimising the degree of mutual frustration. Frustration with your staff may well be the prompt for necessary action.

Jane felt that one of her staff was far too preoccupied with her own interests and did not think through the implications of her decisions for her colleagues. Jane had made this point to this individual on a couple of occasions and had felt ignored. Jane became increasingly dismissive of this individual's contribution because of the frustration she felt about the way the individual contributed to meetings.

A colleague noticed that the relationship between them was frosty and pointed out to Jane that this was having a damaging effect on the wider team. Jane was told frankly by her colleague that if she did not address this situation, the sticky relationship would fester and erode the quality of engagement in the wider team. Jane was slightly stunned by this blunt feedback, but it prompted her into a more direct conversation with the individual concerned.

In practice

- When you feel frustrated about a member of staff, think about what insight that frustration is giving you.

- Be mindful if you let frustration with a colleague fester, as it will affect your working relationship with that individual.

- Be cognisant and responsive when you get feedback from other members of your team that you are showing frustration in relation to an individual.

CLIENTS AND CUSTOMERS

THE CUSTOMER IS ALWAYS RIGHT—up to a point.

The idea

We ignore clients and customers at our peril. Working in the private sector for 15 years means I am acutely aware that a customer is entirely free to decide to purchase coaching from me or to go elsewhere. If a client decides that the time is not right to do some further coaching, there is no point in my becoming frustrated. It is an opportunity to reflect on whether there is learning for me in terms of the coaching approach I bring.

If I become frustrated that a client is not using individual or team coaching as well as they might, I would share that frustration in a gentle way because of my concern that any organisation or individual should use their resources of time and finance well. If I am becoming frustrated that a client is not using my time to good effect, it is right for both parties to explore that frustration.

Sometimes you become frustrated with the customers and clients you are contracted to engage with. As a store manager you may be frustrated with the behaviour of customers. As a doctor you may be frustrated by the way your patients ignore your advice. As a civil servant you may become frustrated when the ministers for whom you work want to take actions that you do not think are consistent with the evidence.

These frustrations will not go away. They are a part of the way leaders in any organisation experience working with diverse clients and customers. Such frustrations can often be creative. They wake us from complacency. When you feel frustrated with clients and customers, you can either sulk and feel hard done by, or face the reality of their reaction and decide on practical steps that turn frustration into progress.

Jane was irritated by the way certain clients did not seem to treat her with respect. They cancelled meetings at the last minute and came ill-prepared. She would often feel that her time and theirs was being wasted. She reminded herself, 'the customer is always right', but felt that the opposite was the reality. The behaviour of some customers through their dismissive approach would sometimes irritate her to the point where she ranted to her colleagues. She needed to be calmed down. Her ranting was exhausting for others and herself. Her frustration was creating deep frustration for others. She knew she had to face into her own frustration about the behaviour of clients and customers, and grow up.

In practice

- Be aware when you are likely to feel frustrated with clients or customers and, metaphorically, walk away from the situation before that situation gets to you.

- Recognise how you can seek to short-circuit the frustration you face when clients and customers do things that you know will irritate you.

- Be pleasantly surprised when a client or customer who normally frustrates you is helpful.

71 SPONSORS

Sᴘᴏɴsᴏʀs ᴀʀᴇ ᴠᴀʟᴜᴀʙʟᴇ but their interest may only be for a season.

The idea

We all benefit from sponsors who have an interest in us and are committed to our success. A sponsor might have been involved in recruiting us to our current role and feel a sense of obligation to help us succeed. A sponsor might have seen us do well in a particular situation and be advocating our cause. They might recognise that we come from a particular background or have personal issues that we are addressing. They recognise that work can be tough and want to help us be successful. A sponsor might be someone who has agreed to be a mentor who shares their perspective with us at periodic intervals.

We may become frustrated that a sponsor is not giving us enough time or helping us enough. A good sponsor keeps an eye on us and provides prompts at good moments, but they are mindful that they need to be impartial in their dealings with us.

A sponsor may be there for a season. They will be using the time they commit to mentoring younger people in a focused way, rationing the amount of time they give particular individuals. You may be frustrated that a mentor is not willing to see you more often; but the mentor may be thinking that you need to make your own decisions and not be dependent on steers from them.

Someone who has appointed you to a role may well be a strong sponsor for a period; but if you don't deliver, that sponsorship might turn into critical action if they feel let down or frustrated by your approach and actions.

When you feel a sense of being let down by a sponsor, recognise that part of that frustration could be a prompt for you to be less dependent on the sponsor and to chart your own path. Sponsorship is great for a season, but both parties need to move on.

When Henry joined a government department as a junior accountant, Alan, the Head of Profession, chaired the panel that appointed him. Alan was very supportive of Henry in his first few weeks and Henry looked forward to periodic mentoring conversations. After a while, these conversations became fewer. Henry felt let down by his sponsor, as he was keen to talk through issues with him.

It took a while for Henry to accept that the mentoring conversations had been designed for his initial few months and that Alan was now committing similar time to other new recruits.

A year later, when Alan gave Henry some feedback that he needed to up his game, Henry initially felt aggrieved that his so-called sponsor had been critical. A few days later, he accepted that he needed to take Alan's comments seriously, as Alan was Head of Profession and would have a key voice in developing his career.

In practice

- Recognise those who have an interest in your success and development and build a relationship with them as your sponsors.

- Accept that sponsorship will be for a season and make the most of it while it lasts.

- Recognise you will feel an element of frustration when a sponsor shifts their interest to others.

- Recognise that if you let a sponsor down they can be very critical of you.

72 CRITICS

THERE WILL ALWAYS BE critics whose comments you have to listen to and sometimes respond to, and on other occasions be immune to.

The idea

If someone is being critical of you, you are being noticed. Being ignored is far worse than being criticised. If you are ignored, you are being regarded as an irrelevance. If you are being criticised, you are having an impact, or people would not bother to criticise you.

Being criticised is frustrating. The first question to ask yourself is: what is valid about the criticism? There may well be occasions when the critic is making a good point that you are well advised to take account of. There is no point getting frustrated by criticism that is valid when corrective action is needed.

All feedback and criticism says as much about the person expressing it as it does about the person being criticised. Hence, a second question to ask yourself is: what is the criticism saying about the individual expressing it? When someone is critical, it gives you insights about what is most important to them and how your comments or behaviour are affecting them.

There is always a risk that we take criticism personally and build up a personal dislike of the person expressing the criticism. It helps us maintain our stability if we reframe our reaction in terms of what is the issue the other person is concerned about and how best we respond to their comments about an issue. Depersonalising comments removes any sense of personal vendetta or personal pain.

Often we do not have to keep listening to the voices of critics. We do not have to repeatedly check social media or keep re-reading a critical e-mail. We need to be honest about the sources of critical comments, try to understand them, and think through what our next steps might be—then move on, so that our mind is not full of negative feedback that can send our confidence into a downward spiral.

Henry received feedback that some colleagues in other sections thought he was pedantic. Henry thought he was doing his job meticulously and was frustrated by their pained reaction to his interventions. Henry had not put a lot of effort into building good personal relationships with some of the people he was working with in the other sections. The negative feedback frustrated him.

Henry knew he had to understand their needs more clearly and seek to build a joint partnership with them so that they could address key financial issues together. His initial frustration about these critical comments turned into a determination to build closer and more co-operative working relationships with colleagues elsewhere in the organisation.

In practice

- See criticism as people recognising that you play a valuable role.

- Recognise that criticism says as much about the person offering the criticism as it does about you.

- Seek to depersonalise criticism so you are focusing on the issue alone.

- Be mindful that you need to build a working relationship with critics as much as you do with allies.

73 TURNCOATS

SOME PEOPLE WILL join the opposition. So be it.

The idea

There will always be those people who learn as much as they can from you and then move on and join the opposition. You may have invested a significant amount of time recruiting and developing someone. You may have deliberately put business their way, which has had a detrimental effect on your own business.

But they have not felt the same loyalty to you as you have to them. They have felt a clear conscience in gaining experience from you and then moving on. This can be particularly irritating if they join a competitor that is operating in the same space as yours.

In this situation, you can either be frustrated with their behaviour or be philosophic that this is the nature of the world in which you operate. There is an inevitability that if you develop people successfully they will become marketable and you will lose them. You can point to the greater good this is providing for your particular profession. When you develop a young teacher effectively so they become a Head of Department in a neighbouring school, you may feel that you have strengthened the credentials of a school that is recruiting from the same pool of pupils as your school. On the other hand, you can view your success in nurturing this young teacher as helping to raise the standards of education for pupils across the whole area.

You may justifiably feel frustrated that someone has milked you for your experience and wisdom and is now using it for their own personal and commercial advantage. We have to accept that that is life; it happens. It is difficult to both hold on to our intellectual property and influence another generation for good. If we want to build a legacy of influencing a wide range of different people, we have to accept that we can either describe someone as letting us down by moving on, or see them as an evangelist who is taking forward what we have developed into other spheres.

In his second year in the organisation, Henry took pride in helping to develop a new recruit. He felt that together they would make a good team and would be able to take on interesting projects. After six months the new recruit announced that he was leaving. He had perfectly good reasons for moving to another part of the country where his family lived, but Henry felt that his time developing the new recruit had been wasted.

Henry was frustrated that he had not been forewarned that this move was a possibility. It took a while for Henry to accept that he had learnt a lot through developing this new recruit and that together they had achieved much in a few months. Henry accepted he had to park his frustration and be deliberate about supporting a colleague in the last few weeks in his role, so that his mentoring legacy would be a positive one.

In practice

- Do not expect people to return the loyalty that you have invested in them.

- Accept that people will move on after a season and be looking after their own interests.

- Try to be philosophic when you feel let down by someone who is joining a competitor.

- Think of the greater good you are creating for the wider organisation or profession when you have invested in people and assisted their development.

FAMILY MEMBERS

HANDLING FRUSTRATIONS WITH family members can spill over into a work context in unhelpful ways.

The idea

Our spouse, parents and siblings are very important to us. We want to fulfil our family commitments out of both responsibility and love. We want to be available for family members when they need us. It helps when there are family members with whom we can talk through our different hopes and commitments, but frustration might be only a little way below the surface.

We love our parents dearly, but when they become forgetful and do not remember the frequency with which they call us, we can become frustrated. The occasional emergency call from an elderly parent when we are at work is fine, but repeated calls from someone suffering memory loss can be disruptive to others as well as to ourselves.

When siblings have chosen different life pathways with different degrees of success, there can be an underlying frustration that can easily burst out into aggravation. When spouses or life partners of siblings do not get on well, there is a danger of misunderstanding and discord that can impact our well-being and create frustration at times when we most need calmness and family support.

Family members can be our greatest source of affirmation and encouragement. They can also become a trigger for visceral emotional reactions that destabilise us. The effective approach is different for different people. What seems to work best is a balance between affection and openness between family members, and knowing when to keep a safe distance—with your sources of renewal and support not just being from within a family context. You learn to be realistic about frustrations caused by family members, while keeping your distance and not being over-dependent on their support.

Henry treasured good memories of his parents. He knew they had always been committed to his well-being. After his mother died, he sought to support his father in practical ways and visited him every week. When dementia began to take a grip on his father, Henry recognised that he was already beginning to lose him. When his father began to telephone him asking the same question for the sixth time, Henry became frustrated, but knew he had to hold that frustration at bay and not let it show to his father or his children. Henry knew that the best way of countering his frustration with his father was to spend quality time with his own children. Henry recognised that one day he, too, would need the support and patience of his own children.

In practice

- Treasure the affirmation of family members.

- Have other sources of support, too, so you are not over-dependent on the approval of family members.

- Recognise that apparent disapproval from family members can hit you hard and lead to deep frustration.

- If frustration with a family member might lead you to saying things that you will later regret, seek to walk away from that situation and dissipate your frustration in other ways.

75   YOUR CHILDREN

Always remember that your children will mirror your behaviour, often exhibiting the same frustrations as you.

The idea

Your children are often much more like you than you care to admit. If your reaction to the tantrum of a two-year-old is to shout at them, they are likely to think that shouting at other people is an appropriate behaviour. If you are patient with your children as they work through difficult issues, they are more likely to be patient in addressing problems they face. If your frustration immediately shows, your children will judge it to be acceptable to show immediate frustration, and their frustration will frequently bubble out immediately.

We can get frustrated with the children in our lives for different reasons at different stages. Frustration as parents flows from the constant crying of a child, the tantrums of a two-year-old, the unpredictable behaviour of an eight-year-old or the morose attitude of a teenager. We learn how to accept and handle the frustration that children cause while continuing to love and care for them. The way we handle our frustration with children equips us to handle frustration at work with a wide range of different people.

When an individual is working through how best to engage and work with a member of staff, I might ask them how they would handle that individual if they were a disruptive three-year-old or a rebellious teenager. Often, we have learnt how to handle our frustrations within our family, which can give us techniques when we are dealing with people at work who are exhibiting immature behaviour.

Often the main learning from handling our frustrations with the children in our lives is about patience and timing. There are moments when we want to be clear about boundaries or advice and do that in a thought-through way, not as a result of frustration bursting out of us.

Henry recognised that his parents had dealt with his behaviours as a child in a way that had shaped him going forward. His parents had been clear in their advice that he should not leave education prematurely and should go on to university, but they did not push him towards any particular institution. Henry observed that there could have been moments when his parents became frustrated with him, but they did not let their frustration get in the way of treating Henry consistently with deep love and support. Henry was grateful that his parents did not let their frustration flow out into behaviour they would later regret.

In practice

- Recognise how you handle frustrations with your own children and seek to be consistent in your approach.

- When frustration with your children is obvious, be deliberate in the love you subsequently show them.

- Recognise that how you handle frustration with your children gives you an excellent source of learning about how to handle frustration in other contexts.

HANDLING FRUSTRATIONS WITH POLICIES AND PROCESSES

TECHNOLOGY THAT DOES NOT DO WHAT YOU WANT IT TO DO

IF THE TECHNOLOGY DOES NOT work in the way you want, keep cool and carry on.

The idea

How often have you wanted to sabotage the technology at a workshop or conference? The speaker is completely preoccupied with the technology, trying to get PowerPoint slides projected in the right order. When the technology does not work as they want, the speaker becomes flustered and irritated. Like a contagious disease, everyone in the room becomes irritated. Some speakers seem unable to survive without PowerPoint slides, even though their audience is sinking into boredom.

Some of the best talks I have heard have happened when the technology has failed and a speaker has had to speak from their heart and their memory rather than be dictated to by PowerPoint slides. Sometimes when I speak to an audience I will use just two or three slides, including a minimum of points. On other occasions I rely on stories or a one-page hand-out.

I was feeling frustrated recently when I was the third keynote speaker at a conference where the first two speakers had given worthy, if somewhat dull, talks based on PowerPoint slides. Our topic was how to have influence and impact. I decided to seek to change the tone of the event and departed from my original intent and instead spoke on 'How do you get a three-year-old to eat their carrots?', drawing parallels about influence and impact in different spheres. I heard from a number of participants that this metaphor had impacted them much more than bullet-points on a screen.

When technology does not do what you want it to do or other people's use of technology is causing you and others frustration, it is worth being bold, changing tack and telling stories from which pertinent points can be drawn.

Jenny lived in a culture where PowerPoint presentations were the norm. There was an expectation that these presentations would be colourful and animated. Jenny decided that sometimes she would use a one-page prompt and tell stories. Her aim was to capture the imagination of the people in front of her. If the technology was not working or proving troublesome, she would readily proceed without the technology. She taught herself not to be flustered by the vagaries of technology and would rapidly switch away from using the technology if there were complications.

In practice

- Do not be a slave to the latest technology.

- See technology as part of a repertoire of ways of communicating and influencing people.

- Remember that people will recall visual images and stories far more readily than bullet-points.

- Be wary lest you show frustration when the technology is not working—remember that frustration is contagious.

77 | SPORADIC WI-FI CONNECTIONS

WI-FI IS A WONDERFUL TOOL, but we can become over-dependent upon it.

The idea

When I was an undergraduate, I used to write a letter home once a week. This was part of the routine of life and helped me summarise what I was learning at university and the impact that university life was having upon me. These were attempts at considered, thoughtful letters, which my mother retained and were passed on to me when she died.

Today, we live in a world of instant communication where we expect to express our views in the moment. There are huge pluses which enable family members to keep in touch on a regular basis, with electronic communication being far more like natural spoken conversation than the more formal and considered letters my generation used to write.

When a Wi-Fi connection is broken, we feel bereft, unable to have instant access to information and restrained from expressing our views so that others get the benefit of our instant reflections on a myriad of different subjects. Sporadic Wi-Fi connection can be a good thing. It forces us to think and decide what our considered response will be when the Wi-Fi connection is renewed. A Wi-Fi connection allows much stronger partnerships to be built up quickly between people in different places across the globe. But the speed with which we connect and the expectation it creates about quick responses limits our capacity to be thoughtful in developing our approach and next steps.

A Wi-Fi disconnection may feel immensely frustrating in the middle of a meeting, but it forces us to reflect. It means we have to think about next steps and have some time to do so without being pressurised into an immediate opinion on the current issue of the day.

Jenny was part of an international consultancy working closely with colleagues in India. She had built up a good rapport with her colleagues through the use of frequent Skype calls. Jenny recognised that she had become dependent upon this type of communication. When the Wi-Fi contact became erratic, she had to resort to telephone conversations, which worked just as well.

When the Wi-Fi connection was down for four hours, Jenny's immediate reaction was frustration, followed by the realisation that she needed to spend a couple of hours thinking through the issue they were wrestling with. When the Wi-Fi connection was renewed, she had moved her thinking on and was ready to put forward a proposition. Jenny accepted that on future occasions when the Wi-Fi connection failed she could sit back and not be resentful about the situation. She needed to turn the problem into an opportunity and to think in a structured way about next steps.

In practice

- Be careful that you do not take Wi-Fi for granted and keep refining how to use it well.

- Have an agreed contingency plan for when Wi-Fi is not working.

- Use the periods when Wi-Fi is down to think through next steps and talk with colleagues who are nearby.

- Practise rationing your use of Wi-Fi to reduce your dependence on it.

INTERNATIONAL TIME ZONE DIFFERENCES

See international time differences as providing additional flexibility and not as an overriding problem.

The idea

I work for a few weeks each year in Vancouver, which is eight hours behind the UK. This means I can have meetings which are early morning in Vancouver and mid-afternoon in the UK. When I work with people in Australia, a nine-hour time difference means an early-morning call in the UK is late afternoon in Australia. Global teams get used to this reality and build compensating routines into their working practices.

It can be frustrating that when it is afternoon in Vancouver you cannot talk to anybody in the UK, or if it is afternoon in the UK you are not able to talk to contacts in Australia. These international time zone differences force us to think about when we engage with people in other continents and when we allocate time and space to reflect and develop our thinking.

The frustration caused by time zone differences is, in most cases, manageable. What can be trickier is when you as an individual are spending time in different time zones, with the frustration that your body does not appreciate this disturbance. We are often expected to travel between time zones on the cheapest possible flights with little regard to health and well-being. We can become immune to the need to look after ourselves, and do not give ourselves adequate sleep and rest. The consequences can be far more damaging than we realise. Perhaps it is better to live with the partial frustration of connecting virtually with people from different time zones rather than the long-term frustration of constantly travelling from one time zone to another. Perhaps we should resist the expectation that we can move rapidly from one time zone to another without adequate recovery time.

Jenny assumed that she should be visiting India to have face-to-face meetings with colleagues on a regular basis. The long-travel distance was disruptive for her family, but to establish herself in this role she was putting her work first. Once she got to know her colleagues in India, she began to engage with them more often through Skype or by telephone. Over time she found that this type of communication worked just as well for most topics as face-to-face meetings. It did mean that sometimes she needed to hold meetings at odd times of day, but that worked out fine as many of these meetings she could do from home.

Jenny began to shift the organisation's culture away from excessive international travel to more deliberate decisions about what was the most effective way to engage with key people. When it was necessary to make a long journey across the globe, she was insistent that there was recovery time so she could be at her best in the meetings.

In practice

- Be deliberate in managing the timing of meetings to take account of different time zones.

- Use virtual means of communication to best effect to be compatible with different time zones.

- Be deliberate in using face-to-face meetings when they are appropriate. Do not assume that this is always the best means of communication.

- Be deliberate in ensuring you get enough time to sleep when you are travelling between different time zones.

DIFFERENT INTERPRETATION OF RULES IN DIFFERENT CONTEXTS

UNDERSTANDING DIFFERENT PEOPLE's interpretation of rules reduces frustration when rules appear to be flouted.

The idea

Is a rule an absolute requirement, a guideline or an aspiration? You may have worked in contexts where security and safety rules are seen as absolutes because lives are at risk. If you work in the creative industries you may see rules as guidelines to be followed if they appear helpful. To some, a 30-mile-an-hour speed limit is an absolute that has to be obeyed. To others it is a prompt to keep their speed slower than it might otherwise have been.

If we see rules as guidelines, we get frustrated when we observe others rigidly applying rules. If we see rules as absolutes, then our frustration level rises when we see people deliberately flouting those rules and seeking to operate within a broader range of acceptability.

Most successful organisations have accepted norms about processes and procedures, with the recognition that in exceptional circumstances a rule might need to be broken. If a wall is falling down nearby, you would jump out into the road to avoid the falling masonry, recognising that you would never jump out into the road in normal circumstances.

The rules in any organisation have been put there for a reason. It may be that these reasons are now out of date and that the rules need changing. But rather than just getting frustrated with the rules, it helps to understand why they are there, and then explore the prospect of changing a rule so that it is adapted to meet current circumstances. You might be frustrated by the sequence of security procedures you have to go through in order to access data—but when you see the consequences when sensitive data has been hacked, you might change your view about the importance of these rules.

The organisation in which Jenny worked had clear rules about the handling of sensitive data. She followed the required procedures— well, sort of. She became frustrated with the hoops she needed to jump through to access data. On one occasion she left her mobile phone on a train and had to report its loss. She was interrogated about how she kept data secure and was not entirely convincing in her answers. Her frustration with the organisation's procedures, and the organisation's frustration with her limited regard for security, were comparable. Jenny received a written warning about the way she followed security procedures. She had no choice but to accept that her company's complaint was justified. She needed to get over her frustration about the organisation's security procedures.

In practice

- Assess how you normally view rules that you are expected to follow—are they an absolute, a guideline or an aspiration?

- Accept that your frustration about rules may be your problem, with the rules being fully justified by the need to address risks.

- Be wary of becoming too frustrated at having to follow rules that are seen by an organisation as absolutes.

80 DIFFERENT ACCEPTED LEVELS OF BEHAVIOUR

BEHAVIOUR THAT IRRITATES YOU may be the norm in another organisation.

The idea

In the UK, a number of government departments recruit senior people from the private sector. For these individuals, the starkest contrast about the switch of sector is often about how people interact with one another. They have been used to a competitive and quite cut-throat environment; they say what they think quickly and directly, often in the most robust language. Then they enter the world of the Senior Civil Service, where officials are taught to be measured in what they say and sometimes delphic in their comments. The new entrants from the private sector are frequently baffled by what they regard as elliptical and sometimes even dishonest ways of communicating.

The new recruits from the private sector can be seen as rude and dismissive. The new recruits can see their new colleagues as indecisive and wordy. It takes a skilful team leader to enable people steeped in different working cultures to understand each other and bring out the best in each other.

When I work with teams whose members come from different backgrounds, I often invite them to talk about how the accepted levels of behaviour in the current team differ from those in a previous team—this can lead to a breakthrough in mutual understanding. Often, individuals are deeply frustrated about the behaviour of their colleagues, without appreciating why they behave in the way they do, and without recognising that their colleagues might be equally frustrated with them. Where a team is aspiring to do well, its members will want to reach a consistent level of expectation about behaviour. What can get in the way is on-going frustration about previous interactions.

Jenny worked with some male colleagues who were finding it difficult to adjust to working with a female boss. Their female role models were their mother and conscientious junior staff. They were at risk of treating Jenny as either their mum or a junior official. Jenny decided it was necessary to talk to them about how she would like to be treated as a senior manager.

Jenny suggested that her male colleagues should talk to some of their peers who also worked for female bosses. She was alternately frustrated and amused by their gauche behaviours. She recognised that she could not allow herself to be too frustrated by them, as this would push her into behaving brusquely, which would be counter-productive.

In practice

* Seek to understand why people behave in the ways they do.

* Recognise that if you are frustrated by the behaviour of colleagues, they are just as likely to be frustrated by your behaviour.

* Seek opportunities for open discussion about accepted norms of behaviour.

* Accept that cultural difficulties about behaviours can be quite deep-seated.

LEADING THROUGH FRUSTRATIONS CAUSED BY SPECIFIC PROMPTS

81 | SOCIAL MEDIA CAMPAIGNS

UNBRIDLED AND EMOTIVE COMMENTS expressed via social media can be devastatingly hurtful and need to be filtered out for our own sanity.

The idea

Instant communication through social media has its benefits. We are informed quickly about crises. We can keep up-to-date with other people and events. We can respond promptly if there is a need for support. On the other hand, social media fuels poorly thought-through prejudices. A frenzy of disgust can escalate fast. One person's misfortune can rapidly become the focus of protest from a huge army of people.

A senior leader dealing with a controversial topic used to read the comments on social media. When he was personally named and accused of having views that he did not recognise, he became angry that he had been so blatantly misrepresented. The next time there was a social media campaign that was critical of his actions, he did not look at the social media comments and asked his head of communications to provide him with a short, measured summary of what was being said on social media. In this way he kept in proportion what was being said on social media alongside what he was hearing from other more considered sources.

If you let your frustrations show in your comments on social media, others will feel at liberty to show equal frustration with you. Putting factual comments and new evidence on social media can be a good means of trying to shift a debate without getting involved in emotive and disruptive exchanges. When there are adverse comments on social media, it is important to be clear how many people are holding those views and whether they have credibility with wider constituencies. Seek to be analytic in your approach to social media rather than being overwhelmed by your feelings.

Hazel felt aggrieved that her work as a school inspector was being slated in a social media campaign. She brought a dispassionate and considered approach to her work. She understood schools well and she was businesslike in her approach. She never sought to be rude, while accepting that she was forensic. Some of the social media comments were personal in questioning her experience and competence.

Jenny had been tutored to be prepared for this type of situation and not let it get to her, but she felt a compulsion to keep looking at the social media comments and had to tell herself quite firmly not to do so. She knew she was doing her job well. She was open to constructive feedback after she had visited a school, but was not going to be dictated to by ill-informed social media comments.

In practice

- Sit lightly to social media comments.

- Be systematic in recognising where social media comments come from.

- Avoid getting involved in emotive and disruptive exchanges.

- Be highly selective in what you look at on social media.

82 GOSSIP

GOSSIP PROVIDES USEFUL DATA. Any frustration it creates needs to be turned into a deliberate decision to ignore it or take action.

The idea

In every organisation, there will be gossip about the leadership. When I am coaching senior leaders, I will try to find out what people say about them privately. The words used in gossip are key indicators of how someone is viewed. Positive gossip can build up an individual's reputation. A leader who shows support to someone having personal difficulties will choose to do so discreetly—the result may be good gossip about the care and compassion a leader has shown and the time they have willingly given to support someone in need.

When I hear negative comments about someone I am coaching—that they can be brusque or dismissive—I will talk through these reactions with the individual. They may have deliberately decided to express themselves directly in particular circumstances and do not mind if they are regarded as demanding. On other occasions the perception that they are rude in some situations is an indication that they should adjust their approach if they want to get the best response out of colleagues.

When you hear gossip about yourself, there is little point in getting frustrated. Knowing the gossip provides valuable data and gives you the opportunity to shift the narrative by being deliberate in how you relate to people in response to this gossip. Reducing your frustration about gossip comes from assuming there will always be gossip, and being deliberate in seeking to shift the tone of gossip about you.

Remember to feed good gossip into an organisation when people have done things particularly well. When gossip is negative about someone and you think they are making a positive contribution, it is worth feeding in good gossip about this individual to counter negative reports.

Hazel recognised that the gossip about her was that she was direct and could be forensic in her questioning. In many ways she thought this was a helpful reputation, as the leaders in a school she was about to inspect would prepare properly and be ready to respond to direct questions. She also recognised, however, that such a reputation could mean that the people she was meeting would be anxious and, therefore, not necessarily be giving of their best.

Hazel recognised that she needed to come across as supportive of others and wanting the best for their school. When she met people who she knew would be anxious, she deliberately maintained good eye contact and sought to be warm and encouraging in her initial exchange with them. Hazel was deliberate in summarising at the end of conversations what she had heard so that those she had spent time with felt they had been listened to and understood.

In practice

- See gossip as providing good data while recognising that gossip says as much about the person expressing it as it does about you.

- Distil the gossip about you into points you accept, as well as other points where you want to shift perceptions.

- Do not be too fazed by gossip—accept it as part of life and leadership.

83 CHANGING FASHIONS

FASHIONS COME AND GO. You can be in favour one month and out of favour the next.

The idea

You can be in favour and thought of as the most likely candidate for promotion, and then a few months later you are regarded as unlikely to be promoted. You are the same person making a similar type of contribution. You can easily feel frustrated that your star has waned when you had thought it was in the ascendancy. News about us can appear fickle. We could have done three or four things well and have had the sponsorship of key people. Then our sponsor moves on, the context changes and other people excel at tasks that are seen as more significant than what we are doing.

It may be fashionable in your organisation to recruit people with a particular background. You have worked hard to develop a set of competencies and experiences that are relevant for future leadership roles, but those who are appointing now are looking for external expertise—your internal experience does not count as highly as it might have done. Perhaps you are of a certain age, gender or ethnicity and the leaders in the organisation want to have a more diverse leadership. This approach might be in your favour on some occasions and count against you on others.

Changing fashions are a reality in any organisation that cannot be ignored. You have to either embrace some of the fashions or demonstrate such distinctive excellence that your candidature will still be strong even though the fashion is to appoint someone with different skills.

You can often respond to changing fashions in a constructive way. If gaining experience serving a charity is seen as useful for your career advancement, that can be addressed. If an organisation is looking to promote people who can engage effectively with young people, that expectation can be addressed. But there is little point in getting too frustrated if an organisation is determined to change its diversity balance and you do not fit the particular categories where they want to increase representation.

Hazel observed an emerging trend that those favoured for promotion tended to speak in an assertive way. Because the organisation needed to move its agenda forward quickly, more reflective leaders seemed out of favour. The choice for Hazel was: should she become more assertive and try to be a stronger presence in meetings; or should she try to deploy her powers of reflection more effectively?

Hazel decided to use the approach of asking key questions in meetings and not being fobbed off when they were not addressed properly. She always put her questions in a way that demonstrated that she wanted to move the business forward. She forced a degree of reflectiveness and reassessing of the evidence—this initially slowed progress, but in the long run pushed forward thinking about next steps in a more robust way.

In practice

- Seek to be amused by changing fashions and try not to be upset about trends you cannot do anything about.

- Anticipate the effect of changing fashions and accept you may need to go with those fashions.

- When you are seeking to contribute in a way that is counter to prevailing trends, be clear about the reasoning for your contributions so that others do not think you are being difficult or obstructive.

84 POLITICAL DECISIONS BY OTHERS

Sometimes political decisions by others are a fixed point which we have no choice but to accept.

The idea

In my first career as a senior civil servant, it was a fact of life that the political party in charge would change every few years. In 32 years, I worked for 17 cabinet ministers, each of whom had different political and policy priorities. I recognised that every two years there was likely to be a shift in political direction, either because a new political party was in control or a new cabinet minister was in post. I was trained not to allow myself to be frustrated by the reality that having worked on a policy for a period, that policy could now be taken in a different direction. This was good training for the rest of life, where changes outside one's control can have an impact on priorities or the extent to which one's contribution is appreciated.

The 2014 Scottish independence referendum and the 2016 Brexit referendum were examples of where the result was close, with nearly half the electorate in each case feeling frustrated by the outcome. Many public servants had worked hard to make the European Union arrangements work effectively for the UK—they now had to do a U-turn and contribute to unpicking their previous work. Inevitably there was inner frustration for some, which needed to be countered by recognition of the significance of the referendum result and the need for professionalism in doing the job they were paid to do.

In commercial organisations, the board might make a decision to change direction, strongly influenced by their reading of the broader political context. When they explain their reasons carefully, it is easier for employees to accept the rationale and move on from their frustration.

The organisation Hazel worked for had decided to outsource more work to India. It was a strategic decision based on an economic rationale. Hazel wanted to support the growing business in India, but did not want to undermine her European colleagues. She felt an element of frustration but knew that many of her European colleagues would feel this more acutely. She was clear that she needed a cogent rationale for the decision, with evidence that in the long term it would benefit all aspects of the business.

Hazel had to work through her own frustration so that she could be genuine and persuasive in seeking to minimise the frustration felt by her European colleagues. She knew they would go through a frustrating time, but as a leader she felt an obligation to give them the data to allow their rational selves to temper their emotional reactions.

In practice

- Recognise the reality of political decisions and their implications.

- Seek to anticipate what political decisions might be taken and how their outcomes might impact on you.

- Be realistic in thinking through which political decisions you can influence and which are fixed points.

85 | MISLEADING COMMUNICATIONS

MOST HEADLINES PORTRAY a single viewpoint. Always look beyond the headline words.

The idea

We become frustrated by emotive headlines and press stories. News editors are seeking to sell their newspapers and can use phrases that are a gross distortion of the truth. After a particular judgement by the UK High Court in 2016, the three judges who made the decision were branded in some newspaper headlines as 'enemies of the people'. Many people were appalled by this crass and emotive treatment. Some national newspapers regard themselves as having the right to castigate others with limited regard to the evidence or the impact of their words. At least most national newspapers employ feature writers who seek to put forward a more balanced perspective.

The press coverage of the Archbishop of Canterbury's speech at the TUC annual conference in 2018 focused on the passage where he discussed Amazon's tax receipts. The rest of the speech was a thoughtful statement about the importance of partnership and moving forward constructively, recognising the learning from past mistakes. One of the benefits of the internet is that it is normally possible to get hold of the full text of a speech after the media has chosen to highlight just one or two elements in a provocative way.

When you feel frustrated by communications within your organisation, it is always helpful to seek to understand the reasoning for that communication and whether the way it has been communicated has accurately represented the intent. Often, our emotional reactions mean that we only hear part of the communication and become frustrated, without looking at the full wording or seeing the wider context.

Initial communications in Hazel's organisation about the offshoring of work to India focused purely on the short-term economic benefit for the firm. The words were drafted by the commercial department, with little regard for how they might be interpreted. Hazel knew that serious thinking had gone into the future development of work in Europe and how the skills of staff in Europe could be used in a different way going forward.

Hazel pressed for more of this rationale to be communicated, so that people's initial frustration could be countered by a recognition that the development needs of staff in Europe were not being ignored. Hazel recognised that she needed to be more persistent in making this point so that the communication was not just about one aspect of the story. She held in mind the quote from English playwright George Bernard Shaw that 'the single biggest problem in communication is the illusion that it has taken place'.

In practice

* Think about how a communication is going to be received by others and what frustration triggers it might set off.

* Recognise the importance of the judicious use of evidence in communications, so that the rational brain has data to help it keep its emotional reactions within bounds.

* Ensure aims are clearly communicated at the start of a process and not just as an optional extra at the end.

86 EMOTIONAL OUTBURSTS

EMOTIONAL OUTBURSTS OFTEN do more damage to the individual having the outburst than the target of the outburst.

The idea

As a 25-year-old member of the private office of the Permanent Secretary of a UK Government department, I was taken aback by an emotional outburst from a Director. The reason he was angry with me was because I had asked him a factual question, which he considered impertinent. I was surprised and shocked by the outburst. I took comfort in the fact that other people had suffered from his 'ire' on a regular basis. Because of his tendency to have emotional outbursts he was treated warily, with colleagues being reluctant to trust him. This individual rarely built sustainable partnerships because colleagues felt cautious with him and frustrated by his unpredictable behaviour.

You may be frustrated by the emotional outbursts of colleagues, but others might be more negatively affected than you. Apprehension about an emotional outburst may cause someone to freeze and look ineffective. When you are frustrated by someone's behaviour, others might be much more frustrated or damaged by it; hence it is important to illustrate to the perpetrator of emotional outbursts the effect that such behaviour has on the confidence and competence of others.

Observing the effect that emotional outbursts can have in damaging someone's reputation gives us valuable forewarning if we are at risk of an emotional outburst. The best of leaders know when they are at risk of saying something they might regret and are willing to call a coffee break or change the subject to give themselves time to cool down. Emotional outbursts create escalating frustration, where your desire to unblock something through frank discussion can rapidly lead to the erection of barriers and delay hopes of progress.

Henry found it frustrating working for a boss who was kind and generous one minute and petulant the next. The unpredictable behaviour of this boss was a constant cause of frustration. It had been flagged up in frequent 360-degree feedback processes, but Henry's boss shrugged his shoulders and did not appear to change his approach.

On one occasion, when Henry was the recipient of a particularly blunt outburst, he suggested a couple of days later that he and his boss went out for a walk at lunchtime. As they walked briskly through a park, Henry began to talk about how his boss's outbursts limited the effectiveness of the team. Henry said that a couple of key members of the team were likely to leave if the boss failed to temper his approach. Henry was unsure whether these words would have any impact, but they needed to be said. Opening the conversation whilst the two of them walked through a park gave his boss the opportunity to voice his reactions and concerns in a neutral environment.

In practice

- When have you suffered as a result of an emotional outburst and when has the outburst enabled you to speak honestly to the individual concerned?

- How do you ensure that you do not fall into the trap of having emotional outbursts that damage rather than help colleagues?

- How can you protect good colleagues from their own emotional outbursts?

FRENZY FOR ACTION

FRENZY FOR ACTION CAN so easily create panic and poorly thought-through decisions.

The idea

There is a grave danger that a leader who is not confident in themselves will want to set off a flurry of activity to demonstrate that they are in charge. This frenzy for action leads to people running around in circles and acting in uncoordinated and often counter-productive ways. Every leader needs a foil that will hold up a mirror to them and help calm them down. Other than in the most extreme circumstances, there is always time to reflect for a few moments and stand back from the fray.

When there is a risk of a frenzy for action, someone needs to ensure key questions are considered about what are the underlying issues, what does success look like and what are the practical steps that are most likely to lead to the desired outcomes? Forcing a measured approach to addressing an issue before setting off a flurry of activity means a much greater likelihood of considered and coherent steps being taken.

When you feel frustrated by the frenzy of action, sometimes you have no choice but to go along with it while keeping a cool head and calm demeanour. You have to choose your moment to raise questions about the direction of travel or the actions that have been initiated. It is about choosing when to call for reflection. This might be during a natural break, when one step has been completed.

If something has gone wrong, an opportunity might present itself to look again at the approach. When you are feeling frustrated, remember that others might be even more frustrated. Knowing how frustration is affecting others will provide an opportunity to help calm down the frenzy for action and move towards a more deliberate sequence of next steps.

Your frustration in having to handle the frenzy for action from others can help give you the resolve to speak up in situations where a frenzy is having a counter-productive effect, while recognising that your timing and the way you present your points are going to be key.

The IT project that Henry was part of was not going well. His boss kept asking for new action to be taken to address these problems, with the result that solutions were being layered upon each other. Henry suggested that the team should have a half-day stocktake outside of the office. Henry's boss agreed to this suggestion more quickly than he had expected.

Having the discussion in a different location with enough time to reflect helped create a much more positive atmosphere than Henry had expected. The mood of the half-day was measured, with team members talking openly about which actions were working well. Henry thought that they could be at a breakthrough point. He was delighted that he had turned his frustration into the suggestion for a half-day away day.

In practice

- When there is a frenzy for action, be careful lest you get caught up in the whirlwind.

- Beware lest you create a frenzy for action which is purely a result of you having thought things through quicker than others.

- When you feel frustrated by the frenzy for action in others, recognise why they are acting in the way they are and be deliberate in seeking to influence their situation in a way that they are going to find helpful.

THE UNEXPECTED

Handling the unexpected is part of the joy and frustration of leading well.

The idea

If every leadership journey was predictable, there would be the risk of boredom. Unexpected events can both dampen our enthusiasm and keep us stimulated by the opportunities that our role provides us with. The more curious we are about what is going to happen in unpredictable ways, the easier it is to keep alert to unexpected events or comments.

If someone's behaviour is surprisingly negative, we can either be frustrated by it or be curious as to why they are taking a particular line. On other occasions someone might unexpectedly agree with us, which vindicates our persistence and patience in setting out our case clearly.

As you look a week ahead, it can be helpful to have a frame of mind whereby you are expecting one good unexpected thing to happen and, say, three negative unexpected things to happen. You are then alert to where there might be a positive opportunity you had not expected. If only two things go wrong in a particular week, then you can describe it as a good week, as your benchmark had been for three things to go wrong.

When you feel deeply frustrated by an unexpected event, it is a reminder that you cannot predict the attitudes and approaches of different individuals. You need to keep a focus on what you believe are the right next steps, taking account of the unexpected, but not being overwhelmed by the unexpected. Sometimes events happen which mean that your job is at risk. In these circumstances do not allow yourself to be thrown into a slough of despondency. It may be a moment for thinking about different possibilities for the future. Perhaps you needed a shock to jolt you into fresh thinking about your own next steps.

Henry was shocked when it was announced that two directorates were going to be merged together. This development had not been anticipated. Henry's first reaction was that this merger would not help his career. He had built a good reputation for himself in his current area and was shortly to meet key milestones on a couple of projects.

Henry was at risk of being thrown by the uncertainty of the effects of the merger. He oscillated between frustration and dejection, with the risk that his resilience would be undermined. Thankfully a couple of good friends jolted him into thinking that there could be opportunities flowing from this merger—it was not all bad news. Henry recognised that how he handled the unexpected depended a lot on his frame of mind. Was he going to let the situation undermine his resilience or help renew his determination?

In practice

- Is your natural reaction to be frustrated or intrigued by the unexpected?

- How regularly can you bring a frame of mind whereby you look forward to the unexpected rather than be daunted by it?

- How much can your sense of curiosity allow you to be intrigued by the unexpected and then enjoy engaging with the resulting opportunities?

DISCOURTESY AND RUDENESS

Discourtesy and rudeness are to be abhorred, but we might be too sensitive sometimes.

The idea

We can be affronted if someone is discourteous or rude to us. We think that their behaviour is outrageous and contemptible. We might be at risk of turning one poorly thought-through and disrespectful comment into a major slight. It could have been that the individual was preoccupied or stressed and did not express themselves in a way that they would normally have preferred.

On the other hand, rudeness that goes unchecked can become insidious. You may be able to handle the rudeness and brush it off, but others might feel the rudeness more acutely. Rudeness that is not checked can be permanently demeaning as well as disrespectful. Good levels of courtesy bring out the best in people. A lack of courtesy results in people's confidence being undermined and a sense of hopefulness squashed.

We can often feel frustrated on behalf of other people when we see them treated with discourtesy or rudeness. We want to stand up for individuals or groups who are not being treated with respect. We want to demonstrate that we care about individuals whose efforts and goodwill are being disregarded.

There may be times when we regret our failure to stand up for proper levels of courtesy and respect. Rather than regretting the past, the question is: how do we respond when we observe rudeness and discourtesy being inflicted on others? Does our frustration lead to quiet seething, or choosing a moment to intervene? Perhaps it means building an alliance with others who are also concerned about discourteous and destructive behaviour.

Henry was unnerved at the discourtesy and rude approach of the Finance Department. He thought the attitudes displayed were unhelpful and unprofessional. There was a complete absence of politeness in the way the finance people treated others in the organisation—it was as if power had gone to their heads and they thought they were in an unassailable position.

Henry got to know a peer in the Finance Department and asked how he viewed the way they engaged with other parts of the organisation. This colleague looked embarrassed by the question and admitted that he did not feel comfortable with the way his colleagues treated other departments. Henry and the Finance colleague decided that they would model a different way of engagement that was based on constructive partnership. They sought to model a way of working between departments that was professional, direct and realistic, with a shared prospectus about an agreed set of purposes. This approach defused Henry's frustration, and began to change the climate in which Finance worked with other parts of the organisation.

In practice

- Accept that sometimes discourtesy is an accidental by-product rather than an intended slight.

- Be ready to find ways of addressing discourtesy and rudeness before they become the norm in an organisation.

- Recognise that your own frustration at the rudeness of others should not lead to your being equally rude in return.

90 AN OUTBURST OF HATE

SOMETIMES HATE CAN SPILL OUT and cannot be ignored.

The idea

An outburst of hate is in a different league from discourtesy and rudeness. Sometimes the pressure of a particular situation or a focus on getting something done can lead to a discourteous or rude attitude. But an outburst of hate is something more visceral, where there can be deep resentment about someone's ethnicity, background, culture, religion or gender.

When hate surfaces, we can be shocked and sometimes numbed by that shock. The rush to judge a particular category of people irrespective of their personal qualities flows from a deep-seated hate that should have no place in a civilised society. When we see hate, we are right to be alarmed. In recent history there are too many examples of genocide for us to brush aside the risks of hate exploding in a world fuelled by social media. Hate can be insidious as well as overt. Groups may talk benignly about other categories of people and then demonstrate behaviours that are premeditated and unscrupulous.

It is right to be frustrated into action by those who show hate. It is also right to be mindful that some people might hide behind an assumption that they are the objects of hate. Those who describe themselves as the perpetual victim may be exaggerating the sense of hate and using that as a reason to be unwilling to engage openly with people of a different viewpoint. Sometimes you may be dealing with people's frustration because of the hate exhibited by different groups, but on other occasions the frustration might be because people are interpreting events as hateful when that interpretation is a misplaced exaggeration.

Henry had been brought up in a Catholic family in Northern Ireland. During his childhood, there were members of his community who expressed hatred towards Protestants. When he began work in London, he was surprised that he found his colleagues equally easy to work with, whether they were Muslim, Protestant or Catholic. Hating those from a different religion had been deeply embedded in his psyche. He had fought hard to overcome this derision of those belonging to a different faith from his own.

Henry was very sensitive to any hint of intolerant behaviour. He could sense a hint of hate in someone's demeanour or language. As a consequence, he worked hard to build constructive partnerships with colleagues from different faith groups. He had seen outbursts of hate in his childhood. He was going to do his level best to create harmony in the workplace, with any hint of hate being addressed before it gained traction.

In practice

- Be shocked when you see hate and aggression expressed.

- Be deliberate in identifying and addressing hateful words and actions.

- Allow your frustration to lead to decisive action when you observe hate.

SECTION L
KEEPING COOL
THROUGH FRUSTRATION

LEARN HOW BEST TO PUT EVENTS INTO PERSPECTIVE

It CAN BE HELPFUL to look back and reflect from a wider perspective on the relative importance of an event.

The idea

Sometimes we can be completely preoccupied with an immediate issue. We are thrown into disarray by an unexpected event. We are either stunned into inactivity, or go into overdrive, magnifying the destructive consequences of a localised incident. It is so easy to turn a setback into a major crisis. With the benefit of hindsight, many doom-laden events have passed without huge consequence. As we look back, we can see we have built them up out of proportion and wasted a lot of emotional energy.

On the other hand, there are occasions when we do not fully appreciate the significance of particular events. I have led workshops where there has been a breakthrough. A new level of mutual understanding has been reached. Competitors have suddenly accepted that they can achieve far more together than in opposition to each other. One of my tasks when I coach teams is to create a context where there can be breakthroughs, with participants then accepting that they are going to look to the future with a very different perspective and a new level of mutual understanding.

It is important for the team members to see the wider context and not just be dominated by the immediate tactical considerations. When aggravation is building up because of very different viewpoints, it helps if that growing aggravation can be viewed as an indicator of a deeper issue that needs to be resolved about longer-term objectives and how people work together effectively.

Marcia used to get very het up when the Executive Team questioned the analysis in her proposals. She felt intimidated and sometimes even bullied. A good friend encouraged her to think about the pluses about this questioning. It demonstrated that the Executive Team was interested in her area and wanted to ensure it operated successfully. Marcia was reluctant to accept this constructive interpretation of an interrogation she did not enjoy.

Marcia recognised that she needed to strengthen the team and thought the Executive Team members would be dismissive of this request. The opposite was the case, as they recognised that her project was of particular importance to the organisation. A couple of the Executive Team members suggested some highly regarded individuals from their areas as potential candidates to work in Marcia's team. This generosity enabled Marcia to recognise that she was held in high esteem and need not be frustrated about how she was viewed by the Executive Team.

In practice

- Recognise when the passage of a few days puts an apparently big incident into a different perspective.

- Recall how some events of minor significance have been breakthroughs and led to a key change of direction.

- Practise looking back on a week to see how best you put various events into perspective.

BE COMPASSIONATE TO YOURSELF AND OTHERS

WHEN FRUSTRATION BURSTS OUT, seek to be compassionate to yourself and not add fuel to the frustration.

The idea

When a team reviewed how they worked together, one of their conclusions was that the team's members needed to be more compassionate to each other and to themselves. The team members set high expectations, both for themselves and for each member of the team. There was a relentless focus on raising performance. This emphasis on making a difference in society was why members of the team were hugely committed to their work. But their conversations could become intense and their expectations of each other highly demanding.

The team explored what it would be like if they were more compassionate to each other. They did not want to drop their standards. They believed it was right that discussions were challenging, with the focus on continuous improvement, but that did not mean they had to be relentlessly robust with each other. They were never rude or angry to each other—they recognised the dangers of intemperate behaviour, but there was a relentlessness about the demands they put on each other, even though they were for the best of reasons.

The team decided that being compassionate to each other involved understanding even more clearly the underlying concerns of individual members. It meant recognising when someone was addressing an overlay of issues where they would benefit from practical encouragement and support. Being compassionate with each other was not about being soft—but it was about being considerate, thoughtful and showing practical kindness.

When you feel frustrated, what does it mean to be compassionate to yourself? It might mean creating a bit of space to think, or taking some physical exercise, or negotiating a change of deadline so that your 'to do' list becomes more manageable. It might mean saying no to certain requests.

Marcia was conscious of the pressures on the Executive Team and why they were putting demands on her. She had tended to view them as blinkered and at risk of being unrealistic. She decided that she could view them in a different way and see them as needing compassion rather than disdain. For Marcia, compassion was about an attitude of mind and about practical steps. She decided that she would seek to build a stronger personal relationship with some of the team and find out more about what they were interested in. She sought to discover what made them laugh and what helped them relax and look at issues in a less forensic way. She discovered that a couple of them could be teased, and would respond using metaphors to illustrate situations they were facing rather than just tables and facts.

In practice

- See the exercise of compassion as a sign of strength and not weakness.

- Exercise compassion alongside hard-nosed realism.

- See practical acts of kindness as akin to oiling the gears to enable them to work smoothly.

- Know in what ways you need to be kind to yourself and be willing to exercise that compassion.

RECOGNISE WHO CARES ABOUT YOUR WELL-BEING

ALLOW PEOPLE TO CARE about your well-being. It is in no one's interest for you to be continually exhibiting macho behaviours.

The idea

Depression has often been called the curse of the strong. Those who bring a single-minded, determined approach can get through an immense amount of work with impressive speed. They can look indestructible as they take on one seemingly impossible task after another. They keep pushing forward unstintingly. They seek to persevere through tiredness and anxiety, with the risk that all of a sudden their confidence collapses and their self-esteem is gone. The strong need colleagues and others to care about their well-being just as much as those with vulnerabilities.

The more frustrated you become and respond with 'I can do even more', the greater the risk of exhaustion. We all need people who recognise when frustration in us reaches a point where we are at risk of going 'pop' or becoming irrational in our decisions. It can be useful to ask a good colleague to keep a careful eye on your well-being and to be frank with you if you show signs of taking things out of proportion.

There does need to be some caution about why people care about your well-being. For some, there might be a desire for favouritism or some sort of return on their investment in you. Those who really care about your well-being will not have an ulterior motive. Without being unnecessarily suspicious, it is always worth keeping an eye on why someone is showing care for your well-being, and not being taken in by overtures where there might be some ulterior motive.

Marcia kept telling herself that she loved a crisis. She was able to make quick decisions and build alliances when urgent action was needed. She described herself as a 'crisis junkie' and was always volunteering to work in areas where there was a crisis, or an impending crisis. She did not look for support from others and did not particularly notice if people thought to care for her. She got a shade irritated if people asked her if she was working too hard.

When she was laid low with a bug, Marcia was conscious that her energy levels were not picking up quickly. She surprised herself by hoping that people would ask her how she was. For the first few days nobody did, which made her frustration about her lack of recovery worse. Marcia decided that she needed to demonstrate a bit more care for the well-being of her colleagues. If they were feeling similar to her, they would benefit from a bit of care and attention. The change of attitude to her colleagues was soon reflected in them asking her how she was. She recognised that caring for each other's well-being flowed out of a sense of mutual support.

In practice

- Do not be dismissive of those who express care for your well-being.

- Be willing to share how good colleagues might express their care for you.

- Demonstrate care for others in the way you would like them to care for you.

- See it as your prime responsibility to care for your own well-being.

REMEMBER THAT OTHERS MAY BE EVEN MORE FRUSTRATED THAN YOU

THERE IS NO PARTICULAR MERIT in monopolising frustration.

The idea

I observed teams when I worked in the UK Government who would compete with each other to express their levels of frustration. The degree of indignation kept rising, as one person's emotive language was outdone by another. It sounded as if the world was coming to an end, trumped by the belief that the universe was about to be terminated.

Perhaps we can play a role in de-escalating frustration rather than winding people up to be more frustrated. This does not mean being unrealistically reassuring and implying that someone's frustration does not matter. But it might mean helping them to see issues from different perspectives and put their frustration into a wider context. Sometimes we have to let other people talk their frustration out—but there may be a moment when we can help them look at the sources of their frustration through a different lens. Perhaps giving them your sole attention when having an informal conversation, or going on a brisk walk with them, will help them work through their frustration to the point where they can begin to smile about their own reactions.

In the heat of the moment, when frustration is burning within us, we can be blinded to how others are experiencing frustration and not recognise how much it is exhausting them. When we are frustrated, the lens through which we view others can become cloudy and we can lose touch with how others are handling similar issues.

When a team is frustrated, it is important to observe in colleagues when their frustration levels might be at risk of reaching danger point, leading to impetuous judgements, or the shutting out of key information, or the exhibiting of unpredictable patterns of behaviour in relationships or the excessive consumption of alcohol.

Marcia worked closely with two colleagues, one of whom was far more laid-back than Marcia, while the other seemed to get frustrated at the slightest provocation. At least with the second person Marcia had early warning of their feelings. She assumed that her colleague who appeared laid-back was not frustrated with the relative slowness of the project they were engaged on, but all of a sudden this person's frustration burst out in a moment of anger. Marcia had misread his behaviour and had not appreciated that frustration was building up in him that could explode into a destructive reaction.

Marcia decided that the three of them should talk openly about what caused them frustration and how they handled their different levels of frustration. They agreed that it was important that they were able to give each other early warning if there was a risk that frustration could reach a point where it led to unhelpful and potentially destructive behaviour.

In practice

- Seek to calibrate what triggers frustration in your colleagues.

- Have a compact whereby you are open with colleagues about the level of frustration you are experiencing and how best others can enable you to handle that frustration with care.

- Be especially cognisant of those who look laid-back but for whom frustration can gradually build up and then explode.

KNOW HOW BEST YOU 'LET OFF STEAM'

WE ALL NEED A MEANS OF expressing our frustration in a way that releases pent-up aggression but does not have a destructive effect on others.

The idea

Someone who was seen as a model of calmness occasionally needed to go for a long walk and would, in an empty field, shout out very strongly his views about people and situations. He needed to verbalise his aggression to get it out of his system. In everyday life he never used swear words. When shouting at the top of his voice in a field he was uninhibited in his use of graphic language. Having had his rant, this individual returned calm, collected and in perfect control of himself.

I can often hear the frustration level in someone's voice as the pitch becomes harsher and they talk more quickly and often repetitively. I seek to create a situation where people can express their frustration up to the point where they are able to shift their focus into a more reflective and then constructive conversation.

For many people, they need a mechanism for working through their frustration from one context before they enter another context. I sometimes worry about people who have become very frustrated during the course of one meeting before moving on to the next. An urge to visit the local pub immediately after a frustrating meeting can be a danger sign for some people; or, equally, it can for others be their measured method of handling their own frustration.

When you feel frustrated, physical activity can help you handle that frustration in a way that means you release pent-up energy and then refocus on how you re-enter a situation with purpose and calmness.

Marcia recognised that when she got frustrated she needed to have a good rant. If she could rant at someone for 15 minutes uninterrupted, she would feel a lot better. Marcia's colleagues recognised that she needed to process things by talking them through. They were patient with her because they saw the benefit of her ranting through issues.

There was some feedback that perhaps she could rant a little less often and not at such great length. Her colleagues did not expect Marcia to stop ranting, but wanted to encourage her to put some boundaries around her ranting by gently suggesting that long rants might be counter-productive to everyone involved.

In practice

- Observe how others 'let off steam' in order to handle their frustration.

- Share with close colleagues how best you defuse your frustration and allow them to help you do that effectively.

- Be careful lest you judge people for letting off steam in ways that you would not regard as appropriate.

- Be deliberate in finding ways that work for you in defusing your frustration, but be mindful when this is best done in private rather than in public—there might be a field where you can express verbal protests in splendid isolation.

KNOW HOW TO RELAX AND WHAT REFRESHES YOUR THINKING

WHEN WE KNOW HOW to press the relax button, even when frustration levels are high, it can make a big difference to our well-being.

The idea

When we are very busy, the idea of relaxation seems unrealistic and inappropriate. If our team members are working hard, we feel guilty if we take a break. Perhaps our colleagues need us to take a break so that we are better able to cope with the frustrations of the moment.

Relaxing the body might involve brisk walks, a gentle stroll, a visit to the gym or a run around the nearest park. When I worked on employment and tax policies at the UK Government Treasury, I had the privilege of working in a building adjacent to St James's Park. If I wanted to think issues through, a quick walk around the park was helpful. The Foreign Secretary at the time (Douglas Hurd) could often be seen walking briskly around St James's Park with a small entourage surrounding him as he used the park as a venue for 'on the move' meetings.

We all have different means of refreshing our body, mind and soul. All three are important so that we keep fresh physically, mentally and spiritually. This allows us to be as clear as possible about what is most important in the approach and contribution we are seeking to make.

A question that is worth asking yourself on a periodic basis is: what refreshes your thinking? Your response might relate to what you read or who you engage with in conversation. Who, or what, helps you view issues in a fresh way? Who lifts your thinking about what is possible? What enables you to tackle a frustration with new resolve?

Vince could become very dour in a busy period. Frustration was etched on his face. His determination cascaded through the team, who wanted to support him. But that unswerving resolve could be exhausting for both him and his team. A couple of Vince's colleagues knew that part of their role was to tease Vince. They knew how to make him smile and not take himself or a particular situation quite so seriously. When Vince became too intense, one of his colleagues would take him out for a cup of coffee. When his frustration began to show in unreasonable demands, they knew it was time to encourage him to take a brisk walk in the park.

In practice

- Build moments of relaxation into your working day.

- See relaxation as essential to your well-being and not an optional extra.

- Be deliberate in looking after your physical, mental and spiritual well-being.

- Enable others to help you press the relax button when your frustration begins to have detrimental effects.

PARK A FRUSTRATION FOR A PERIOD AND THEN RETURN TO IT

NOT ALL PROBLEMS NEED to be resolved immediately. The passage of time may turn a seemingly intractable problem into a manageable irritation.

The idea

As leaders, we feel conscious that it is our duty to solve problems. When problems look intractable, frustration builds up and it becomes more difficult to address the issue in a measured way. Often it is more productive to say to yourself that you will return to a particular frustration at a time of day or week when you would feel best equipped to deal with it. Creating a time lag gives an opportunity for the subconscious brain to work through an issue. We have all known situations where we started with bafflement about an effective way forward and a day or two later there was greater clarity in our mind about next steps.

Parking an issue for a period enables you to be open to different insights that might be relevant to addressing that issue. We may end up in conversations with people who can provide a new angle or draw on their previous experience. We do not normally observe how many red cars we see, but if we consciously look for red cars we notice a lot of them.

Similarly, we may not normally be observing how others deal with particular issues, but if we become deliberate in observing how they handle a particular type of situation, then we will be processing information about what works well or otherwise for others in similar situations to our own. Parking a frustration for a while and then returning to it helps put that frustration into proportion. We may conclude that it is less of an issue than we had initially thought; or on reflection we conclude it is more fundamental, with decisive action being needed.

There are moments when continuing to park a frustration is not the right step. Just as it is helpful to say that you are going to return to a frustration at a predefined time, it can be unhelpful if this becomes a regular excuse for inaction. It can be helpful to say to yourself that I must reach a conclusion by a specific date, but in the interim I will be open to different insights and approaches gleaned from others.

Vince regularly became frustrated that he was not receiving clear instructions from his boss. He knew that to demand clarity in an e-mail was not helpful and would be ignored. He needed to choose his moment to talk through issues with his boss. He needed to prepare the way by saying that at their next meeting he would like to work through a couple of specific issues. Vince also recognised that his own frustration with the boss's apparent limited interest was unhelpful. When this frustration began to surface, he knew he had to park it and then seek to address the issue in a conversation with his boss that needed to be as relaxed as possible.

In practice

- Be deliberate in choosing the most productive times of the week when you can best address frustrations.

- See the resolve to delay handling a frustration to a defined time as a strength.

- Be mindful if you are perpetually parking a frustration and ignoring it.

- Be deliberate in encouraging your subconscious thinking to be working through frustrations and be open to linking together different information and insights.

98 REMEMBER THOSE WHO HAVE KEPT THEIR COOL THROUGH BIGGER FRUSTRATIONS THAN YOURS

Observing how others stay cool through frustration can help you stay cool through your own frustrations.

The idea

One Director General I worked for experienced a period of being criticised in a national newspaper. Throughout this period he kept a clear focus on what being professional meant in his day job. Whatever the external noise, he maintained focus through being clear about what were the professional things to say and do. This helped him block out the inevitable emotional angst that comes from seeing oneself berated or caricatured in the media. As a senior civil servant, you are not in a position to answer back. You have to keep your cool and not be diverted by the machinations of media speculation.

You may realise that close colleagues are having to deal with frustrations concurrently in their work and family lives. Someone who is dealing with frustrations flowing from the declining health of parents or difficult behaviour of teenagers may be handling frustration on a number of fronts at the same time. Perhaps the work environment involves frustrations that are more transitory than those in family life.

Observing how someone keeps their cool and professional focus through a myriad of frustrations gives insights into the sources of their underlying values and resilience. Insights into what enables those we admire to be utterly professional can encourage us to reaffirm and reinforce our own values and sources of resilience.

Vince admired one of his close colleagues whose wife suffered from depression and who had two children who were behaviourally challenged. This colleague's family life was demanding and relentless. He had very little time to himself. Coming to work was a respite. Dealing with very difficult family circumstances meant that this colleague handled frustrations at work with amazing equanimity. He was able to tackle issues one step at a time and not let other people's frustrations get on top of him.

Vince recognised even with his colleagues that there were moments when his frustration was at risk of showing through—it was at these moments that this colleague always seemed to be suggesting a coffee break.

In practice

- If colleagues share personal information with you, recognise the mix of frustrations they are handling across their lives.

- Watch how others keep professional and focused, whatever the frustrations placed on them inside or outside work.

- Be deliberate in adopting approaches that other people use to keep calm.

- Be willing to suggest a coffee break when you or others may be in danger of losing your cool.

SAY 'HALLELUJAH ANYWAY'

WHATEVER IS GOING ON, however frustrating, you can say 'Hallelujah anyway'.

The idea

When I was an undergraduate student at Durham University, I led a group of students who ran holiday clubs in Devon. I worked closely with the Vicar of Cullompton, who had a sign on the notice board in his study saying, 'Hallelujah anyway'. When you sat opposite the vicar, the words 'Hallelujah anyway' were positioned above his head. This phrase has stayed with me ever since. It is relevant, whether you come from a faith perspective or not, to be able to celebrate life whatever is going on around you.

Celebrating life for some is about praising God. For others, celebrating life is about recognising we each have purposes and opportunities in our lives. Tragic and unpredictable events can damage and even devastate that sense of celebration of life. But even after destruction there can be new life. The field or forest may look devastated, but there will always be new shoots even if they take a long time to germinate.

Whatever the devastating effect of frustration might be, if we keep looking for signs of hope or new life, we can be uplifted by possibilities. There may be an element of cynicism within us that hope is vain and illusory, but if we have no hope our enthusiasm for life and the future dies. Sometimes we have to say to ourselves, 'Hallelujah anyway'. We need to keep pushing through frustration with the belief that there can be green shoots and there can be new life. All is not lost, however acute the frustration or dire the apparent devastation.

Vince felt like he was bashing his head against a brick wall. The Finance Department would not give him enough resources, while the HR Department was slow and mechanistic when it came to recruitment. His peers did not appear interested in what he was trying to do. The expectations upon him were unrelenting. There was not a lot to celebrate.

Vince knew he must not sink into despondency and cynicism. He would celebrate the smallest of steps forward. He talked brightly about glimmers of hope. He made certain that all members of the team were aware of progress and positive feedback in different parts of their territory. He would not naturally use the phrase 'Hallelujah anyway', but when a colleague repeated this phrase to him, it summed up his approach. Vince did not resist this description of the attitude he was trying to bring to frustrating circumstances.

In practice

- However big the frustration, seek to identify some signs of progress that you can highlight.

- Remember how you can best celebrate small successes amidst big frustrations.

- Use a phrase like 'Hallelujah anyway' to help you bring a sense of perspective and celebration amidst difficult circumstances.

REMEMBER THAT THERE IS A NEW DAY TOMORROW

KEEP REMEMBERING THAT there is a new day tomorrow, however frustrating today has been.

The idea

Those of us who are parents may remember conversations with our children when they have had a bad day. We seek to help them look forward to the following day by referring to good things that are planned or people they will meet. For the youngster, the encouragement might be about who they might walk to school with, what they might eat for lunch or what might be in store at the end of the school day.

In doing this, we seek to open up the possibility of a good day tomorrow. Perhaps the day has been painful, with scrapes or tears. As a parent, we are alongside them, empathising with their pain but seeking to enable them to embrace the possibility of a better day tomorrow. We want to lead them gently into possibilities and away from their pain.

There are parallels for us too. At the end of a day, our frustrations may have exhausted us or wound us up. The prospect of the next day may well be gloomy if we are dealing with more of the same. But a new day brings new conversations, different information and the possibility of edging forward. Tomorrow we will have new energy, our brain will have processed more data and linked together different insights.

A new day could mean new shoots, new conversations and new possibilities. If we hold on to that possibility, then we will be ready to see green shoots, new insights and opportunities. If we enter a new day thinking that our frustrations will destroy us, then they probably will. If we enter a new day thinking that we have to live with our frustrations and there will always be new insights that affect those frustrations, then we are more likely to handle the challenges of tomorrow with our heads held high rather than with gloom eating up our hope and joy.

Vince found it difficult to accept the view of one of his colleagues that there was always a new day tomorrow. The unrelenting enthusiasm of his colleague seemed incompatible with the reality that Vince faced, but Vince noticed that this colleague was able to handle frustrations well and did not let a never-ending sequence of frustrations burn him out. This colleague had a long-term perspective that enabled him to see each day as a new opportunity rather than a new threat.

Vince recognised that when he talked with the children in his life, he was helping them to be realistic about their frustrations and to see each day as a new beginning. He brought a positive enthusiasm to his family life that he sometimes found difficult to replicate in his working life. Vince recognised there was an apparent dichotomy here and that there would be merit in applying to his work persona the same approach he adopted with his children: by encouraging colleagues to see tomorrow as a new day and not just a re-run of the previous day.

In practice

- Observe whether you bring a different approach to encouraging people to think into the possibilities of a new day in different spheres of your life.

- Observe how you encourage children and young people to move from a frustrating day into a new day.

- Hold firm to the belief that there is a new day tomorrow with new possibilities.

- Whilst some frustrations may feel terminal, remember that when you enter a new day, some frustrations may feel less acute.

BOOKS BY PETER SHAW

Mirroring Jesus as Leader. Cambridge: Grove, 2004.

Conversation Matters: How to engage effectively with one another. London: Continuum, 2005.

The Four Vs of Leadership: Vision, values, value-added, and vitality. Chichester: Capstone, 2006.

Finding Your Future: The second time around. London: Darton, Longman and Todd, 2006.

Business Coaching: Achieving practical results through effective engagement. Chichester: Capstone, 2007 (co-authored with Robin Linnecar).

Making Difficult Decisions: How to be decisive and get the business done. Chichester: Capstone, 2008.

Deciding Well: A Christian perspective on making decisions as a leader. Vancouver: Regent College Publishing, 2009.

Raise Your Game: How to succeed at work. Chichester: Capstone, 2009.

Effective Christian Leaders in the Global Workplace. Colorado Springs: Authentic/Paternoster, 2010.

Defining Moments: Navigating through business and organisational life. Basingstoke: Palgrave/Macmillan, 2010.

The Reflective Leader: Standing still to move forward. Norwich: Canterbury Press, 2011 (co-authored with Alan Smith).

Thriving in Your Work: How to be motivated and do well in challenging times. Singapore: Marshall Cavendish, 2011.

Getting the Balance Right: Leading and managing well. Singapore: Marshall Cavendish, 2013.

Leading in Demanding Times. Cambridge: Grove, 2013 (co-authored with Graham Shaw).

The Emerging Leader: Stepping up in leadership. Norwich: Canterbury Press, 2013 (co-authored with Colin Shaw).

100 Great Personal Impact Ideas. Singapore: Marshall Cavendish, 2013.

100 Great Coaching Ideas. Singapore: Marshall Cavendish, 2014.

Celebrating Your Senses. Delhi: ISPCK, 2014.

Sustaining Leadership: Renewing your strength and sparkle. Norwich: Canterbury Press, 2014.

100 Great Team Effectiveness Ideas. Singapore: Marshall Cavendish, 2015.

Wake Up and Dream: Stepping into your future. Norwich: Canterbury Press, 2015.

100 Great Building Success Ideas. Singapore: Marshall Cavendish, 2016.

The Reluctant Leader: Coming out of the shadows. Norwich: Canterbury Press, 2016 (co-authored with Hilary Douglas).

100 Great Leading Well Ideas. Singapore: Marshall Cavendish, 2016.

Living with never-ending expectations. Vancouver: Regent College Publishing 2017 (co-authored with Graham Shaw).

100 Great Handling Rapid Change Ideas. Singapore: Marshall Cavendish, 2018.

The Mindful Leader: Embodying Christian wisdom. Norwich: Canterbury Press, 2018.

Forthcoming books

Leadership to the Limits: Freedom and responsibility. Norwich: Canterbury Press, 2020.

Booklets

Riding the Rapids. London: Praesta, 2008 (co-authored with Jane Stephens).

Seizing the Future. London: Praesta, 2010 (co-authored with Robin Hindle-Fisher).

Living Leadership: Finding equilibrium. London: Praesta, 2011.

The Age of Agility. London: Praesta, 2012 (co-authored with Steve Wigzell).

Knowing the Score: What we can learn from music and musicians. London: Praesta, 2016 (co-authored with Ken Thompson).

The Resilient Team. London: Praesta, 2017 (co-authored with Hilary Douglas).

Job sharing: A model for the future workplace? London: Praesta, 2018 (co-authored with Hilary Douglas).

The Four Vs of Leadership: Vision, values, value-added and vitality: An enduring framework. London: Praesta, 2019.

Copies of the booklets above can be downloaded from the Praesta website.

ABOUT THE AUTHOR

PETER SHAW has coached individuals, senior teams and groups across six continents. He is a Visiting Professor of Leadership Development at Huddersfield, Chester, De Montfort, and Surrey Universities, and is a Professorial Fellow at St John's College, Durham University. He has been a member of the Visiting Professorial Faculty at Regent College, Vancouver since 2008. He has been a Visiting Professor at the Judicial College in Melbourne, and at the Vancouver School of Theology. He has written 28 books on aspects of leadership; some have been translated into seven different languages.

Peter's first career was in the UK Government, where he worked in five Government Departments and held three Director General posts. Peter has been a member of governing bodies in higher and further education. He is a licensed lay minister (Reader) in the Anglican Church and plays an active role in the Church of England at parish, diocesan and national levels. He is a Lay Canon of Guildford Cathedral and Chair of Guildford Cathedral Council.

Peter holds a doctorate in Leadership Development from Chester University. He was awarded an honorary doctorate at Durham University for 'outstanding service to public life', and an honorary doctorate by Huddersfield University for his contribution to leadership and management.

In his coaching work Peter draws from his wide experience both as a leader and as a coach to leaders in many different contexts. He seeks to bring insights into his coaching work with individuals and teams that are underpinned by his Christian faith and understanding. His focus is about enabling individuals and teams to step up in their effectiveness so that they have a clear vision about what they are seeking to do, apply the values that are most important to them, know how to bring a distinctive value added and recognise their sources of vitality.

Peter finds time to reflect when on long-distance walks, of which he has done 30. Recent ones include the Machu Picchu trail, the Lady Anne Way, the Weardale Way, the Cotswolds Way, the Peak District Limestone Way, the Nidderdale Way, and the North Yorkshire Moors Inn Way.